Crafting Luxurious Soaps: Art, Science, and Scent

Handmade Beauty for Everyday Use

Samuel Harper

Table of Contents

INTRODUCTION

The art of soapmaking is an age-old craft that combines creativity, scientific knowledge, and a deep appreciation for the natural world. Every civilization in history, from the ancient Egyptians and Babylonians to the artisanal craftspeople of today, has recognized the importance of soap in terms of personal hygiene and care. But beyond its practical use, soap is a medium for artistic expression, a sensory experience that enhances daily routines with beautiful forms, textures, and fragrances. Soap is a medium that gives rise to artistic expression. In this day and age of mass manufacturing and manufactured items, the art of making soaps by hand is not only a celebration of personal creativity and self-care, but it also represents a return to simpler and more genuine ways of living.

"Crafting Luxurious Soaps: Art, Science, and Scent: Handmade Beauty for Everyday Use" is a book that is intended to serve as a guide for you as you embark on the gratifying adventure of producing your own soaps. This book has something to teach everyone interested in soapmaking, whether you are just starting out and want to learn the fundamentals or you are an experienced soap maker who wants to extend your talents. You will learn how to blend art, science, and aroma in order to create gorgeous handmade items. The primary aim of this course is to teach you how to make luxurious, high-quality soaps that are as appealing to the skin as they are to the senses.

Making soap is an art form that goes beyond simple formulae; it involves knowing how different components interact with one another, how different fragrances mix together, and how visual factors such as colors and textures may convert your soaps into something truly remarkable. Throughout the course of this book, you will be guided through the fundamentals of soapmaking, which will help you understand the science that lies behind the process while also providing you with a wealth of creative ideas. The chemical reaction that transforms oils into soap is called saponification, and you will learn how to safely handle lye, which is the essential component that makes the magic happen. You will also learn about the crucial role that saponification plays.

One more essential aspect of soapmaking is selecting the appropriate components, and in this section, we will delve further into the many oils, butter, and natural additives that have the potential to elevate the quality of your soap to a higher level. From healthy carrier oils such as olive and coconut to sumptuous ingredients such as shea butter and cocoa butter, you will learn how the texture, moisture level, and lather of the finished product are affected by each individual component. In addition to this, you will delve into the world of essential oils and learn how to create one-of-a-kind fragrance profiles that are tailored to your preferences and the requirements of your skin.

It goes without saying that the process of creating soap is not only about science; it is also about creative expression. You will find techniques and advice for making visually attractive soaps with swirls, layers, and elaborate designs throughout the entirety of this book. You are going to learn how to include natural botanicals, herbs, and exfoliants in your products so that they have additional advantages and enhance their appearance. You'll be equipped with the equipment and the knowledge necessary to make something genuinely unique, whether you're producing a straightforward bar of soap for everyday use or a complex bar of soap for giving as a gift.

This book is based on the concept that the process of producing soap can be a highly satisfying and contemplative activity. It is a technique that encourages creativity while also fostering sustainability and mindfulness. Handmade soaps provide you the ability to control what you put on your skin, which allows you to avoid harsh chemicals and reduce waste by choosing natural ingredients that are beneficial to the environment. When you have finished reading this book, you will not only be able to manufacture beautiful soaps, but you will also have a greater understanding of the craft and the potential it has to enrich your day-to-day life.

Now, let's embark on this creative trip together, where the worlds of science and art collide and where aesthetics and functionality coexist.

CHAPTER I

The Science Behind Soapmaking

What is Saponification?

There is a chemical process known as saponification that is responsible for the transformation of oils or fats into soap and glycerin. This reaction is essential to the process of creating soap and serves as the basis for each and every bar of soap that is produced. Saponification is a transition that takes place when a fatty acid combines with an alkali, often sodium hydroxide (commonly known as lye), to produce soap and glycerol. This reaction is the fundamental characteristic of saponification. In order to become an expert in the skill of soapmaking, it is necessary to have a solid understanding of saponification, which is the process that dictates how the various components join together to form the final result. Although saponification may appear to be a straightforward chemical process, it is really influenced by a wide range of parameters. These factors include the characteristics of the fats and oils that are employed, the accurate measurement of lye, and the conditions that are present when the reaction takes place.

Saponification takes place at the molecular level when triglycerides, which are fats and oils composed of fatty acids and glycerin, are broken down by the lye into fatty acid salts (soap) and glycerol (glycerin). Triglycerides are created when fatty acids and glycerin are combined. The highly caustic substance known as lye serves as a catalyst for this process, causing the bonds that keep the triglycerides together to be broken. The molecules of soap that are produced as a result are amphiphilic, which means that they possess both hydrophilic (so they attract water) and hydrophobic (so they resist water) qualities.

It is because of this dual nature that soap is able to bind with both water and oil at the same time, which enables it to effectively remove dirt and oils from the skin as well as other surfaces.

The first step in the saponification process is the creation of a lye solution, which is achieved by combining lye with water. The chemical reaction is then triggered by the combination of this solution with oils or fats. The selection of oils is of utmost importance in the process of soapmaking due to the fact that various oils possess diverse fatty acid compositions, which in turn influence the attributes of the finished soap. For instance, olive oil is used to make a gentle soap that is nourishing and has small bubbles, but coconut oil is used to make a soap that is more robust and has a thicker lather. It is the combination of oils that a soap maker selects that is referred to as the "soap formula," and it is this combination that defines the hardness, lathering ability, and moisturizing attributes of the completed product.

During the process of manufacturing soap, the liquid starts to thicken as the lye solution is combined with the oils as it is being mixed. The point at which the oils and lye have created an emulsion and saponification has begun in earnest is referred to as the "trace," and it is named after the term. As the soapmaking process progresses, reaching trace is an important stage because it signifies that the components are starting to come together to form a stable mixture. With the soap having reached the trace stage, it is possible to incorporate additional components, such as scents, colorants, or exfoliants, without causing the chemical reaction to be disrupted. The process of saponification continues even after the soap has been placed into molds, as the soap "cures." The soap will become more solid and any surplus water will evaporate while the leftover lye will be completely neutralized as the curing process progresses. It may take anywhere from four to six weeks for the soap to cure, depending on the formulation of the soap and the method that is employed.

The use of lye in the saponification process is one of the essential components of the process; nevertheless, it is also one that sometimes leads to misunderstanding or anxiety, particularly among those who are just starting out in the soapmaking industry. As a result of its caustic nature, sodium hydroxide, often known as lye, is a powerful base that must be handled with considerable caution. The inappropriate use of this substance might result in chemical burns or damage to surfaces. Lye, on the other hand, is entirely neutralized throughout the saponification process when it is utilized appropriately and in suitable ratios. This neutralization leaves behind no trace of the caustic properties that it has in the beginning. It can be concluded from this that the final product is completely risk-free for usage on the skin. Every bar of soap, whether it is created professionally or by hand, goes through the process of saponification, which ensures that it does not contain any lye by the time it is ready for use. This is the reason why the worry that handmade soap includes lye is partially baseless. It is essential to have a thorough understanding of how to safely handle lye, which includes the use of protective gloves and eyeglasses, mixing it in an area with adequate ventilation, and adhering to accurate quantities. This will guarantee that the soapmaking process continues to be both safe and successful.

To varying degrees, the process of saponification is essential to the production of various types of soap. Soapmaking using the cold process and soapmaking using the hot process are the two basic procedures that approach the saponification process in slightly different ways. When producing soap using the cold method, oils, and lye solution are mixed together at room temperature or slightly above it. The saponification reaction takes place gradually over the course of many weeks as the soap cures. This technique is used by a vast number of artists because it enables them to exert a greater degree of control over the components and the overall appearance of the finished product. The capacity of cold-process soaps to retain delicate scents or essential oils, which may be lost in higher heat techniques, is one of the most distinguishing characteristics of these soaps. Other characteristics include their smooth texture and detailed designs. However, because cold-process soap must be allowed to cure for a considerable amount of time, users will need to exercise patience until the soap is suitable for use.

The application of heat during the hot phase of soapmaking, on the other hand, increases the rate at which the saponification process occurs. The soap mixture is heated using this technique, which commonly involves using a slow cooker or cooking it on the stovetop. This method speeds up the chemical reaction. As the soap "cooks" and thickens, it eventually reaches a stage that is referred to as the gel phase, which is characterized by the mixture becoming translucent. The soap is placed into molds after it has been cooked, and it may be used considerably sooner than soap made using the cold process. This is because the saponification process is largely finished by the time the soap is molded. When opposed to cold-process soap, hot-process soap has a texture that is typically rougher and less smooth. However, it is ready for use much sooner than cold-process soap. Not only that, but the intense heat that is utilized in this technique has the potential to sometimes lessen the effectiveness of colorants or scents.

Both techniques are based on the same fundamental principles of saponification, yet the final products might be quite different from one another in terms of texture, appearance, and the amount of time it takes for them to cure. Soap makers have the ability to adjust their approach based on their objectives if they have a grasp of how saponification works in both cold and hot process soapmaking processes. The choice between cold and hot process soapmaking is mostly a matter of personal preference and the product that is wanted.

Saponification is an interesting process because it allows for customization, which is one of the most exciting elements of saponification. Soap makers are able to produce a wide variety of soaps with a variety of qualities by utilizing a wide variety of oils and additives in their production process. For example, a soap maker might decide to utilize a higher percentage of coconut oil in order to produce a bar that has a greater amount of lather, or they might choose to incorporate shea butter due to the moisturizing properties that it possesses. All of these variations are accommodated by the saponification process, which results in soaps that may be customized to meet the requirements of particular skin types or preferences. It is possible to further improve the final product by incorporating additives such as essential oils, clays, and botanicals. These additives can provide additional benefits such as scent, exfoliation, or characteristics that soothe the skin. Because of its versatility, saponification is a great procedure for the creation of individualized, handcrafted soaps that go beyond the scope of simple cleansing.

The role that saponification plays in the production of glycerin, which is a natural byproduct of the process, is another significant component of saponification. Glycerin is a humectant, which means that it draws moisture from the surrounding air and assists the skin in maintaining its level of hydration. It is common practice for commercial soap producers to eliminate glycerin from their goods in order to prepare them for usage in lotions or other cosmetic items. This practice can result in soap that is more dryer to the skin. On the other hand, handcrafted soaps keep their natural glycerin, which makes them more delicate and moisturizing than commercially produced soaps. Handmade soaps are frequently believed to be superior to mass-produced alternatives because they provide a more opulent and nourishing experience for the skin. This is one of the primary reasons why handmade soaps are thought to be superior.

There is also a connection between the saponification process and the quality of the water that is utilized in the soapmaking process. Although it may appear to be a straightforward component, the quality of the water and the minerals it contains might have an impact on the final product of the soap. It is common practice for soap makers to utilize distilled or demineralized water in order to prevent unintended reactions between the minerals found in hard water and the components of the soap. These reactions can ultimately result in soap that is less effective or has an unpleasant texture. It is essential to have water in order to dissolve the lye and to assist in the emulsification of the oils; nevertheless, water evaporates during the curing process, leaving behind a bar of soap that is solid and stable. The amount of water that is used in a soap recipe can also have an effect on the amount of time it takes for the soap to cure and how hard it is. While a lower water concentration can result in a more difficult bar of soap being produced in a shorter amount of time, a higher water content may cause the curing process to take longer.

Both the amount of water used and the temperature at which the saponification process is carried out can have an effect on the final result. For the purpose of ensuring that the lye solution and oils are present within the acceptable range when they are combined, soap makers are required to exercise strict control over the temperature of their ingredients. The soap may "seize," or become overly hard if the components are heated to an excessively high temperature, which will make it difficult to manipulate. It is possible that the saponification process will be slowed down if they are too cool, which will, therefore, result in a soap that takes longer to trace or cure. While some soap makers advocate working at higher temperatures in order to speed up the process, others prefer working at lower temperatures in order to have greater control over the texture and design of the soap. Another factor that determines whether or not soap goes through the gel phase is the temperature at which it is produced. The gel phase is a step of saponification in which the soap becomes transparent and heats up from the inside out. It is possible to improve the color and hardness of soap by allowing it to reach the gel phase; however, some soap makers prefer to avoid this situation in order to preserve particular visual effects or textures.

Another important component in saponification is the influence that time plays in the process. Although the first chemical reaction between lye and oils takes place in a very short amount of time, the entire curing process takes a significantly longer amount of time. While this is going on, the soap will continue to harden as any extra water evaporates, and any lye that is still present will be completely neutralized. When soap is allowed to cure for a longer period of time, it becomes more gentle and more durable, which can improve its lather and its lifespan. The majority of cold process soaps require a curing time of four to six weeks; however, some soap makers opt to cure their soaps for even longer in order to obtain a bar that is more solid and has a more refined lather. One of the distinguishing characteristics of handmade soapmaking is the patience that is necessary for the curing process. This patience ensures that the finished product is of the greatest possible quality.

This process, known as saponification, is not only essential to the production of soap but also provides a glimpse into the wider realm of chemistry. When soap makers have a greater grasp of the molecular interactions that take place during this process, they are better able to appreciate the metamorphosis that takes place when simple materials are joined to create something completely new. Because of this information, soap makers are able to experiment and innovate by modifying their recipes in order to obtain particular results or to investigate new methods. The principles of saponification serve as the basis for every successful soapmaking venture, whether the goal is to produce a bar of soap that is soft and suitable for sensitive skin or a bar of soap that produces a high lather for shaving.

To summarize, saponification is a process that involves the transformation of oils and lye into soap and glycerin. This process is both sophisticated and accessible. Craftspeople are able to manufacture a wide variety of soaps with a variety of diverse textures, fragrances, and qualities thanks to this essential component of the soapmaking trade. There are a number of factors that go into the final product, including the selection of oils, the management of lye, the regulation of temperature, and the patience that is required for curing. Because they have mastered the principles of saponification, soap makers are able to develop rich, individualized soaps that are not just great cleaners but also expressions of creativity and caring for their customers. As the popularity of soapmaking continues to rise, the art and science of saponification continue to be as vital as they have ever been. It provides an infinite number of opportunities for individuals who are interested in making beautiful, handmade soaps that can be used on a daily basis.

Essential Ingredients: Oils, Lye, Water

Oils, lye, and water are the three fundamental components that are required for the production of soap. These three components serve as the basis upon which all handmade soaps are constructed. When it comes to the process of saponification, which is the chemical reaction that converts oils and lye into soap and glycerin, each of these components plays an important part in the progression of the process. In spite of the fact that the fundamental idea of soapmaking, which is to combine oils with a lye solution in order to produce soap, may appear to be simple, the intricacies of these components and the ways in which they interact are vast and complicated. When soap makers have a comprehensive grasp of oils, lye, and water, they are able to manufacture high-quality, tailored soaps that cater to specific requirements, ranging from the lather and texture of the soap to its ability to moisturize and cleanse the skin.

Oils are likely the most crucial component in the production of soap because they are responsible for determining a significant number of the final attributes of the soap, such as its hardness, lather, and ability to moisturize the skin. The molecules that makeup fats are long-chain molecules that are formed of fatty acids. Oils are categorized as fats. Lye, when mixed with these fatty acids, results in the formation of the fundamental components of soap. The fact that various oils include a variety of fatty acids is what gives each oil its own set of characteristics that are distinct from those of other oils. In order to attain a mix of hardness, lather, and conditioning in their soaps, soap makers often employ a combination of oils included in their formulas.

Olive oil is one of the oils that is utilized most frequently in the soapmaking process. Olive oil, which is well-known for its ability to moisturize, is typically used to make a soap that is mild, nourishing, and has a creamy lather. Oleic acid is a monounsaturated fatty acid that adds to the moisturizing and softening properties of soap. It is found in high concentrations in this product. Castile soap is a classic form of soap that originates from the Castile region of Spain. Olive oil is often the primary ingredient in Castile soap. When compared to soaps manufactured with other oils, soap prepared with pure olive oil can provide a bar of soap that is softer and produces less foam. Furthermore, olive oil soap is particularly hydrating. Because of this, soap makers frequently combine olive oil with other oils in order to produce a soap that is well-rounded and provides both moisture and a thick lather during the production process.

Because of its capacity to produce a bar of soap that is both firm and has excellent lather, coconut oil is another essential component in the soapmaking process. One of the fatty acids that contributes to the washing and lathering characteristics of coconut oil is lauric acid, which is plentiful in coconut oil. Coconut oil soaps are typically more cleaning than other types of soaps, and they produce huge bubbles that are fluffy. On the other hand, soap made from coconut oil can be drying to the skin if it is used in high quantities. Because of this, it is frequently combined with oils that are more conditioning, such as olive or sweet almond oil. Because of its versatility, coconut oil is a common choice in soapmaking. It contributes both hardness and foam to the finished product, making it a favorite among soap makers.

When it comes to soapmaking, palm oil is another oil that is often utilized. It is highly recognized for its capacity to produce a bar of soap that is hard, stable, and has an excellent lather. It is important to note that palm oil contains a high concentration of palmitic and stearic acids, both of which contribute to the soap's hardness and durability. It is common practice to combine palm oil with other oils in order to produce a soap formulation that is well-balanced. Palm oil is a versatile base oil due to its neutral aroma and color. The usage of palm oil, on the other hand, has become contentious as a result of environmental concerns over palm plantations and the destruction of forests. Most soap makers now look for palm oil that is supplied in a sustainable manner, or that is farmed in an ethical manner. Alternatively, they may use alternative oils, such as shea butter, cocoa butter, or lard, in its place.

Shea butter, cocoa butter, and sweet almond oil are a few alternative oils that are frequently used in the soapmaking process. The shea tree in Africa produces nuts that are used to make shea butter, which is a highly moisturizing substance that also gives soap a creamy consistency. It is abundant in vitamins and fatty acids, both of which are proven to nourish and preserve the skin. Just like shea butter, cocoa butter is a solid fat at room temperature and contributes to the hardness and moisturizing characteristics of soap. Cocoa butter is likewise similar to shea butter. Luxurious soaps that are formulated for dry or sensitive skin frequently contain this ingredient. Soaps designed for sensitive or dry skin frequently use sweet almond oil because of its soft and emollient properties. Sweet almond oil is a lightweight oil that absorbs quickly and is noted for its gentleness.

Because of their skin-conditioning characteristics and the rich feel they provide to the finished soap, these oils are frequently added in recipes despite the fact that they are not utilized as the primary base oils in the majority of recipes.

Animal fats, such as lard and tallow, have been utilized in the production of soap for generations, and they continue to be a favorite choice among traditional soap makers. The bar of soap that is produced from lard, which is formed from swine fat, and tallow, which is rendered from beef or mutton fat, is both hard and long-lasting, and it has a consistent and creamy lather. The soap's hardness and durability are both attributed to the presence of stearic and palmitic acids, which are found in high concentrations in these fats. Animal fats are avoided by some soap makers for ethical or nutritional reasons; nevertheless, other soap makers value the inexpensive cost of animal fats, the availability of animal fats, and the traditional feel that animal fats offer to handcrafted soaps. Using animal fats in soapmaking can be an environmentally responsible choice if they are obtained from farms that are either sustainable or local.

During the process of creating soap, lye is the second most important component after oils themselves. Lye, which is often referred to as sodium hydroxide (NaOH), is a powerful alkaline substance that is used in the saponification process to generate soap by reacting with oils with the oils. In soapmaking, lye plays an essential part because it is responsible for breaking down the fatty acids that are present in the oils and converting them into soap molecules. In spite of the fact that lye is a caustic material that must be handled with caution, it is entirely neutralized during the saponification process, which results in the end product having no trace of the caustic qualities that it initially possessed.

As a result of the fact that each oil needs a particular quantity of lye in order to successfully transform into soap, the interaction between oils and lye is defined by precise measurements. The "saponification value" of the oil is a measurement that changes depending on the type of fatty acids that are present in the oil. This measurement is known as the "saponification value." Saponification charts or soap calculators are utilized by soap makers in order to ascertain the precise quantity of lye that is required for their particular recipe. In a recipe for soap, an excessive amount of lye can produce a harsh and drying soap, while an insufficient amount of lye can leave behind excess oils, resulting in a bar of soap that is either oily or soft. For the purpose of producing a high-quality soap that is not only functional but also kind to the skin, it is essential to strike the appropriate balance between oils and lye.

The idea that the finished soap contains lye is one of the most widespread misunderstandings regarding the process of soapmaking. In actuality, when soap is created properly, all of the lye is consumed during the saponification process, and the end product does not contain any active lye at all. Consequently, despite the fact that it is prepared with lye, handcrafted soap is perfectly safe for use on the skin regardless of its composition. The safety of the soapmaking process is dependent on the precise measurements that are taken and the careful handling of the lye that occurs during the stage of mixing. The process of making soap requires the use of protective gloves and goggles, the mixing of lye in locations with adequate ventilation, and the ensuring that the lye solution is adequately diluted before it is added to the oils.

Water is the third component that is necessary for the production of soap. Before being mixed with the oils, the lye is first dissolved in water, which serves as the medium for the preparation of the mixture. When it comes to creating soap, the ratio of water to lye is particularly significant because it has an impact on the final soap's texture and consistency. It is possible that a soap that contains an excessive amount of water will take longer to cure, will be softer, and will be more prone to cracking. Using an insufficient amount of water can result in the soap mixture becoming too thick, which can make it difficult to pour or manipulate. In order to guarantee that the lye solution is devoid of any pollutants that could potentially disrupt the saponification process, soap makers often make use of water that has been distilled or made through purification.

In addition, water plays a part in the curing process since, over the course of time, it progressively evaporates from the soap, which enables the soap to become more solid. Because it enables the soap to become more solid and durable over time, the curing process is a key component of the soapmaking process. In the course of the curing process, the soap continues to go through the saponification process, and any surplus water evaporates, resulting in a bar of soap that is more robust and long-lasting. The duration of the curing phase varies both according to the recipe and the method that is utilized; nevertheless, the majority of cold process soaps require a curing period of between four and six weeks before they are ready to be used. Hot-process soaps, which are cooked during the saponification process, often require less curing time than cold-process soaps. This is because a significant amount of water has already evaporated during the cooking step.

Despite the fact that oils, lye, and water are the essential components of soapmaking, the incorporation of additional components can further improve the quality of the finished product. Essential oils, for instance, are frequently used in soap in order to impart smell and to provide aromatherapy benefits and advantages. The oils that are produced from plants retain the natural aroma as well as the medicinal characteristics of the plant from which they were taken. Among the essential oils that are frequently utilized in the production of soap are peppermint, lavender, tea tree, and eucalyptus. Each essential oil has its own distinctive aroma profile and benefits for the skin, and soap makers have the ability to combine a variety of oils to create individualized perfumes and therapeutic effects at their disposal.

It is possible to use other additions to soap formulations, such as herbs, clays, and exfoliants, in order to give texture, color, and extra benefits to the skin. Clays like bentonite and kaolin can help detoxify and cleanse the skin, while herbs like calendula, chamomile, and rosemary are frequently used for their calming and therapeutic effects. Clays also have the ability to assist in cleansing the skin. In order to create a gentle scouring action, exfoliants such as oatmeal, crushed coffee, or poppy seeds are added to soaps. This makes them great for use in body scrubs or facial cleansers because they are very effective. Soapmaking is a versatile craft that enables craftsmen to personalize their goods by incorporating a broad variety of natural ingredients. This allows them to create soaps that are matched to individual skin types, preferences, and particular requirements.

When it comes to the process of creating soap, the interaction between oils, lye, and water is a delicate balance that requires accuracy and attention to detail. Each component fulfills a distinct function and makes a contribution to the overall quality of the finished product on the whole. It is possible for soap makers to create attractive, effective, and luxurious soaps that are both useful and aesthetically pleasing if they have an awareness of the qualities of various oils, the role that lye plays in the process of saponification, and the significance of water in the process of generating a soap that is stable and long-lasting.

In conclusion, the foundation of the soapmaking process is comprised of the essential components of oils, lye, and water. Each of these components plays an important part in the production of high-quality handmade soaps. It is the oils that supply the fatty acids that are required for the process of saponification. These oils also define many of the final attributes of the soap, including its hardness, lather, and ability to moisturize. It is the lye that acts as the catalyst that changes oils into soap, and the accurate measurement of lye guarantees that the result is both balanced and safe. Since water is the channel via which lye is dissolved, it also plays a role in the curing process, which makes it possible for the soap to become more solid and realize its full potential. Therefore, soap makers are able to create rich, individualized soaps that are suitable for everyday use by combining these substances, which gives an infinite number of opportunities for creation.

Common Soapmaking Issues and Fixes

In spite of the fact that it is a creative and fulfilling process, soapmaking frequently presents a number of problems that can be frustrating for even the most seasoned soap makers. It is possible for these typical concerns to have an impact on the look, texture, scent, and performance of the finished soap product. These issues might range from wrong component measurements to unanticipated reactions. In order to achieve results that are consistent and of high quality, it is vital to first understand the underlying reasons for these issues and then implement solutions that are successful. The most typical problems that arise during the soapmaking process are discussed in this section. These problems include trace acceleration, separation, creation of soda ash, discoloration, ricing, and overheating. The section also offers methods that can be used to address these problems. As a result of acquiring an awareness of these obstacles, soap makers are able to not only troubleshoot but also prevent many of the issues that arise during the process of creating soap, which eventually allows them to manufacture luxury handcrafted soaps with confidence.

The phenomenon known as trace acceleration is one of the first problems that soap makers could face. This phenomenon describes the soap mixture reaching trace, also known as thickening, at a faster rate than was originally predicted. In the process of manufacturing soap, the point at which the oils and lye have emulsified and the mixture begins to thicken is referred to as the trace. Because trace acceleration shortens the amount of time that the soap maker is able to devote to their task, it might be challenging to incorporate various ingredients, such as colors, fragrances, and other components. This problem is frequently brought on by a number of circumstances, including the kind of oils that are utilized, the existence of particular essential oils or fragrance oils, or the temperature at which the components are included. Coconut oil and palm oil, for example, are examples of oils that are strong in saturated fats and have a tendency to speed up the trace. In a similar vein, several scent oils contain alcohol or other ingredients that enable the thickening process to be completed more quickly.

It is possible for soap makers to modify their formula by using oils that slow down trace, such as olive oil or sunflower oil, in order to limit the acceleration of trace. Bringing the temperature of the soap combination down to a lower level can also help to lengthen the amount of time it takes to work. Instead of constantly blending the mixture, soap makers who encounter rapid trace should blend the mixture using brief bursts of the stick blender until it is completely incorporated. Additionally, testing fragrance oils or essential oils prior to integrating them into a batch will assist in identifying those that may hasten the process of trace. In the event that trace does accelerate in an unanticipated manner, soap makers can still salvage the batch by rapidly pouring the mixture into molds, but the design and texture of the soap may not be as planned.

Another potential problem that may arise during the process of creating soap is separation. This occurs when the oils and lye solution do not emulsify in the correct manner, which results in a layer of oil being deposited on top of the soap mixture. It is possible for this to occur during the initial stages of soapmaking, particularly if the components are not at the appropriate temperature or if the mixture is not thoroughly blended. When the soap is poured into the mold, separation is frequently observed almost soon after the soap has been poured. This occurs because the oils rise to the surface rather than being integrated into the soap.

Soap makers should make sure that the oils and lye solution are at the same temperature before combining them together. This will prevent the oils and lye solution from separating. In an ideal situation, both should be between 90 and 110 degrees Fahrenheit in order to promote optimal emulsification. To obtain a steady emulsion in a shorter amount of time, it is helpful to use a stick blender rather than manually blending the mixture. If there is a separation of the oils and lye in the soap after it has been put into the mold, it may be possible to re-mix the soap or heat the batch gently in order to bring the oils and lye back together. If the separation is significant, another approach is to rebatch the soap, which involves melting down the soap that has been separated and then recombining it.

A typical problem that might have an effect on the look of cold-process soaps is the presence of soda ash. Lye and carbon dioxide in the air react to produce a white powdery film that is visible on the surface of the soap. This film is the result of the reaction between the two substances.

However, despite the fact that soda ash is not harmful and does not have any impact on the functioning of the soap, it can be detrimental to the beauty of the soap, particularly in bars that are colorful or finely made. During the curing process, soda ash is typically produced. This is especially true for soaps that are permitted to come into contact with air too soon after being poured into molds or in conditions that have a high level of humidity.

Covering the soap as soon as it is poured into the mold is the first step in preventing soda ash from forming. This will reduce the amount of time the soap is exposed to air. Eliminating the possibility of ash formation by covering the soap molds with a lid or wrapping them in plastic wrap is one way to accomplish this. An additional method for preventing soda ash is to spray the surface of the soap with rubbing alcohol immediately after pouring it and then again after twenty-four hours have passed. In the event that soda ash does form, it is typically possible to remove it by washing it off with water or wiping it away with a damp cloth. The removal of soda ash is another method that some soap makers employ. They do this by lightly heating the surface of the soap in order to dissolve the ash without causing any damage to the pattern.

A further difficulty that soap makers frequently encounter is discoloration, which is especially prevalent when fragrance oils are utilized. A great number of fragrance oils, particularly those that contain vanilla, are responsible for the soap turning dark or tan over the course of time. This occurs as a result of the existence of vanillin, a substance that, when combined with lye, results in the coloring of the substance. In spite of the fact that the discoloration does not have any impact on the operation of the soap, it may be undesired for aesthetic reasons, particularly when it comes to the production of soaps that are light in color or attractively intricate.

Soap makers can use a vanilla stabilizer in their products in order to regulate discoloration that is induced by aroma oils. This stabilizer helps prevent or reduce the browning impact. The discoloration can also be used to their advantage by making soaps in such a way that the natural browning complements the image that they are going for. By way of illustration, soap makers can set aside a portion of the soap mixture that does not contain fragrance oil and then swirl it into the portion that is discolored in order to achieve a marbled effect. Alternatively, soap makers have the option of using fragrance oils that do not include vanillin in order to completely avoid discoloration.

By adding certain fragrance oils or essential oils to the soap mixture, soap makers run the risk of experiencing a phenomenon known as ricing. The formation of little lumps in the soap mixture that resemble rice is the cause of this occurrence, which results in the soap having a grainy and uneven appearance. Ricing is frequently brought on by a reaction between the fragrance oil or essential oil and the soap batter. This is especially true when working with oils that include certain aldehydes or other reactive chemicals. The lumps that are present in the soap batter can make it challenging to work with, and they may also cause the finished soap to have a little harsh texture.

In the event that racing takes place, the initial step is to proceed with the process of blending the soap mixture using a stick blender. As the combination is given additional emulsification, the ricing will, in many instances, become smoother. If the lumps continue to be present, soap makers may try heating the soap mixture in a gentle manner. This is because higher temperatures have the potential to assist in breaking down the rice-like clumps. It is possible that the soap will need to be rebatched in order to create a smoother consistency if neither of these approaches is successful. Therefore, in order to avoid ricing in subsequent batches, soap makers should conduct a study on their fragrance oils and essential oils before using them, and they should choose oils that are proven to behave well in cold-process soap.

Because of the exothermic nature of the saponification reaction, the soap can become overheated during the gel phase of the soapmaking process. This can be a problem because the soap warms up during this phase. When soap is heated to an excessive degree, it may develop problems such as cracking on the surface of the soap, bubbling, or eruptions similar to volcanoes, in which the soap mixture expands and flows out of the mold. It is more likely that the soap may overheat if it is insulated throughout the curing process to an excessive degree. This is especially true when the soap is subjected to high temperatures or when certain additions, such as honey, milk, or sugar, are used, which naturally raise the temperature of the soap.

As a precaution against the soap combination overheating, soap makers should keep a close eye on the temperature of the soap mixture and refrain from insulating the soap to an excessive degree while it is in the gel phase. For the purpose of preventing the soap from becoming very heated, some soap makers choose to store their soap molds in the refrigerator or freezer for a brief period of time. In the event that the soap maker suspects that the soap is overheating, they can remove the insulation and allow the soap to cool down naturally. In situations when eruptions similar to volcanoes take place, it is frequently possible to salvage the soap by swirling the mixture back down into the mold and allowing it to resume its gel state.

Incomplete saponification is another typical problem that arises throughout the soapmaking process. This occurs when the soap does not completely transform into a solid bar and instead stays mushy or oily. An inadequate lye-to-oil ratio, insufficient blending, or the use of oils with a high moisture content are some of the potential causes of this issue. Other potential causes include a combination of these components. When the saponification process is not finished, the soap that is produced may have a texture that is slimy, greasy, or crumbly, and it may not develop a suitable lather.

In order to prevent incomplete saponification, soap makers should make certain that their recipes are precisely calculated by utilizing a trustworthy soap calculator and that the appropriate quantity of lye is utilized for each of the oils that are included in the creation of the soap. A good emulsion can be achieved by thoroughly mixing the soap mixture with a stick blender. It is essential to make sure that the soap mixture reaches a stable trace before putting it into the mold. In the event that a batch of soap continues to be greasy or soft, it is possible to rebatch the soap by either melting it down and adding more lye or altering the ratio of oil to lye while making the new batch.

Another problem that may occur is seizing, which is especially problematic when fragrance oils or essential oils are used in the soap combination since they have a negative reaction to the soap. Seizing is a phenomenon in which the soap mixture suddenly becomes thicker and becomes too stiff to work with. This phenomenon typically occurs within a few seconds of the addition of the fragrance oil. Because of this, it may be impossible to pour the soap into molds or to mix colors and other additions into the soap. Seizing is frequently brought on by particular components found in the fragrance oil, such as alcohol or specific reactive chemicals, which mix with the soap batter and cause it to harden before its time.

As soon as the batch begins to seize, soap makers need to take immediate action in order to save it. Despite the fact that the final texture and look might not be optimal, the soap can be scooped into molds as fast as possible if it is still somewhat workable. In the event that the soap has completely seized and cannot be poured, the only possible option may be to rebatch it. The process of rebatching entails melting down the soap that has become seized and then re-mixing it. This provides a second opportunity to include the fragrance oil in a more gradual manner or to opt out of using it altogether. You may assist in preventing seizing by testing fragrance oils before using them in a large batch. Additionally, you can prevent seizing by blending the fragrance oil in by hand rather than using a stick blender. This will prevent the mixture from becoming over-agitated.

The production of soft soap is another common problem, which occurs most frequently when the soap recipe contains an excessive amount of water or when the soap has not been allowed to cure for an adequate period of time at the appropriate time. The use of a high proportion of liquid oils, which do not contribute to the hardness of the soap as much as solid fats do, might also result in the production of soft soap. Soaps that include a high percentage of oils, such as olive oil, for instance, may take longer to solidify and may feel mushy or sticky to the touch for a number of weeks after they have been applied.

For the purpose of addressing the issue of soft soap, soap makers should make certain that the ratio of water to lye in their recipe is accurately calculated and should avoid using an excessive amount of water. The rule of thumb is to use 33 percent water in relation to the amount of oils that are called for in the recipe; however, this can change based on the particular ingredients that are used. In addition, it is essential to let the soap cure for a minimum of four to six weeks in order to achieve a bar that is extremely durable and long-lasting. In the course of the curing process, the water content of the soap evaporates, resulting in the soap being more firm and less harsh. It is also possible for soap makers to integrate more robust oils, such as coconut oil or palm oil, into their formula in order to produce a bar of soap that is more robust from the beginning.

More than one aesthetic problem, glycerin rivers are something that some soap makers have to deal with, particularly when it comes to cold process soaps. An uneven distribution of heat during the saponification process is the cause of these rivers, which appear as translucent or shining streaks within the soap. These rivers manifest themselves as rivers. Although glycerin rivers may not have an effect on the performance of the soap, they may be undesirable for soap makers who are attempting to achieve a smooth and uniform appearance in their bars during the production process.

It is important for soap makers to closely monitor the temperature of their soap combination and to avoid overheating the soap while it is in the gel phase. This will help prevent glycerin rivers from occurring. In addition, lowering the amount of water that is included in the recipe can assist in reducing the production of glycerin rivers. This is because an excessive amount of water can contribute to improper heating. It is common practice to accept the appearance of glycerin rivers as a distinctive visual characteristic of the soap. This allows the bars to have more personality without lowering the overall quality of the product.

Soapmaking is a complex combination of art and science, and even the most accomplished soap makers can face challenges such as trace acceleration, separation, soda ash, discoloration, ricing, overheating, partial saponification, seizing soft soap, and glycerin rivers. In conclusion, soapmaking is a delicate balance of art and science. However, soap makers are able to overcome these challenges and manufacture attractive, high-quality handmade soaps, provided they have a comprehensive awareness of the factors that contribute to these issues and the methods that are most effective for addressing them. To enhance their craft and feel the delight of creating luxury, individualized soaps that are not only useful but also a representation of their artistic vision, soap makers can continually improve their abilities, experiment with different ingredients, and learn from their previous experiences. This allows them to elevate their trade.

CHAPTER II

Ingredients for Luxurious Soaps

Choosing the Right Oils

As a result of the fact that the choice of oils has an effect on the texture, hardness, lather, conditioning capabilities, and even the final aroma of the bar, selecting the appropriate oils for soapmaking is one of the most important decisions that a soap maker can make, this understanding enables soap makers to craft bars that meet their desired goals, whether it be creating a moisturizing soap for sensitive skin, a hard bar for long-lasting use, or a luxurious soap with a rich, creamy lather. Each oil brings its own unique set of characteristics to a soap recipe, and understanding these qualities allows soap makers to craft bars that meet their desired goals. It is not just the fundamental chemistry of saponification that contributes to the intricacy of soapmaking; it is also the artistry of blending oils in such a way that brings out the greatest qualities of each individual component. In this section, we will discuss the many kinds of oils that are typically used in soapmaking, how to successfully balance them in recipes, and the significance of sustainability and ethics when it comes to the procurement of oils.

An expertly crafted combination of base oils is the essential component of any soap formulation. Compositionally speaking, these oils, which are also referred to as carrier oils, make up the majority of a soap's composition and are accountable for the majority of the attributes that soap makers strive to regulate, including hardness, lather, and conditioning. Olive oil, coconut oil, palm oil, and castor oil are all examples of common basic oils. Each of these oils offers a unique set of advantages to people who use them. For instance, olive oil is well-known for its gentleness and the fact that it may treat the skin quite effectively. The process of creating soap results in the creation of a bar that is mild, hydrating, and perfect for those with sensitive skin. On the other hand, olive oil by itself does not produce a bar that has a robust lather, and soaps that are manufactured with a high percentage of olive oil can require a significant amount of time to cure and can be quite soft. As a result, it is frequently mixed with other oils in order to achieve a balance between its qualities.

On the other hand, coconut oil is widely appreciated for its capacity to produce a luxurious, bubbly lather as well as its antibacterial and antifungal properties. When coconut oil is used in the production of soap, it helps to create a bar that not only completely washes the skin but also generates a substantial amount of foam, even when the water is hard. On the other hand, due to the substantial cleansing action that it possesses, coconut oil can be drying to the skin when it is used in large quantities. In order to counteract this, soap makers frequently reduce the amount of coconut oil that is included in a recipe, typically keeping it at a level that is between 20 and 30 percent of the total oils, and blend it with oils that are more hydrating, such as olive or sweet almond oil.

Palm oil, which is another popular base oil, is frequently utilized because of its capacity to produce a bar of soap that is both hard and long-lasting. While palm oil, like coconut oil, helps to maintain a consistent lather, it is not as effective as coconut oil in terms of deep cleansing. The fact that it can give the soap a firmer texture, which makes it more long-lasting and less likely to dissolve fast in water, is the fundamental reason for its popularity. The utilization of palm oil in soap production, on the other hand, has become contentious due to environmental issues, notably those pertaining to the destruction of habitats and deforestation that are associated with palm oil plantations. A significant number of soap makers are currently looking for sustainable sources of palm oil or selecting substitutes like lard, tallow, or other plant-based oils that offer comparable hardness without having an adverse effect on the environment.

Castor oil is another beneficial ingredient that can be added to a variety of soap formulas; however, it is normally only used in very small amounts. In addition to adding creaminess and assisting in the stabilization of bubbles, it is a highly viscous oil that serves to improve the lather of soap. When it comes to creating soap using the cold process, castor oil is especially helpful since it assures that the soap will generate a luscious foam that is thick and creamy and will feel wonderful on the skin. Castor oil, despite the many advantages it offers, should be used in moderation because an excessive amount of it can cause a bar to become sticky or excessively soft.

In addition to these base oils that are frequently used, there is a wide range of specialty oils that can be used in soap formulas in order to improve particular attributes. In the case of soaps, for instance, shea butter is usually included due to the rich and moisturizing characteristics that it possesses. In addition to being rich in vitamins A and E, shea butter is extremely nutritious and has the ability to calm skin that is dry or irritated. When used in a soap formulation, it results in the creation of a conditioning bar that has a luxurious and delicate feel to it. Similarly, cocoa butter is well-known for its ability to harden, as well as its capacity to produce a bar that is not only firm but also conditioned. In addition, cocoa butter possesses a natural smell that is not overpowering and can be used to complement the addition of essential oils or fragrance oils to the soap.

In the soapmaking industry, jojoba oil is another type of specialty oil that is highly sought after due to the distinctive composition it possesses. Jojoba oil, in contrast to other oils, is scientifically classified as a liquid wax, and it bears a striking resemblance to the natural sebum that is produced by human skin. Because of this, it is a good choice for the production of soaps that are very conditioning and mild on the skin. As a result, these soaps are suitable for individuals who have skin that is prone to acne or with sensitive skin. Because of its high cost, jojoba oil is normally only used in very small amounts, yet it gives the soap a smooth and hydrating texture once it has been applied.

Avocado oil is yet another rich oil that can be utilized to impart moisturizing and conditioning characteristics to soap without compromising its quality. Avocado oil is extremely nourishing and is especially beneficial for dry or aging skin because it is comprised of essential fatty acids and vitamins A, D, and E. Avocado oil is rich in all three of these vitamins. Using it in soap results in the creation of a bar that is creamy, conditioned, and has a calming and comforting feel to it. It is possible to use avocado oil either as a component of the base oils or as a super fatting oil, which is added after the saponification process in order to preserve a greater number of the beneficial properties that it possesses.

In addition to using individual oils, soap makers frequently use mixtures of oils in order to create the right balance of coarseness, lather, and conditioning in their products. It is common practice for a well-rounded soap recipe to incorporate a combination of hard and soft oils, with each type of oil contributing a unique set of properties to the finished product. For instance, olive oil is typically used for conditioning, coconut oil is used for lather, and palm oil is used for hardness. This is a common combination. Whether they want a bar that is very moisturizing, long-lasting or creates plentiful lather, soap makers can modify their recipes to satisfy specific demands by adjusting the amounts of each oil. This allows them to create a bar that meets all of their requirements.

Soap makers need to take into consideration the fatty acid profiles of the oils they select, in addition to ensuring that the qualities of the various oils are in harmony with one another. There are many different types of fatty acids, and each form of fatty acid offers a particular set of qualities to the soap. Fatty acids are the fundamental components of fats and oils. For instance, the bubbly, cleaning lather that is produced by coconut oil and palm kernel oil is due to the presence of lauric and myristic acids, which are found in high amounts in both of these oils. Having said that, these fatty acids have the potential to cause drying effects on the skin, which is why they are frequently balanced with oils that provide more conditioning.

Oleic acid, which can be found in oils such as olive oil and avocado oil, is known for its ability to condition the skin and is also known to be kind to the skin. For those with sensitive skin, soaps that are high in oleic acid are typically gentle but hydrating, making them an excellent choice. The hardness of the soap is a result of the presence of stearic and palmitic acids, which are present in hard fats such as tallow, palm oil, and cocoa butter. These acids also contribute to the creation of a bar that is not easily broken. A rich sensation is imparted to the soap by these fatty acids, which also contribute to the creaminess of the lather.

Linoleic and linolenic acids, present in oils such as sunflower oil, hemp seed oil, and grapeseed oil, are polyunsaturated fatty acids that give extra conditioning qualities. However, soaps manufactured with large quantities of these oils might be prone to oxidation, leading to rancidity. To prevent this, soap makers often employ antioxidants such as vitamin E or rosemary extract to stabilize the oils and lengthen the shelf life of the soap.

Considerations of ethics and sustainability are also taken into account when selecting oils for soapmaking, in addition to the functional properties of the oils themselves. As people become more aware of the problems that affect society and the environment, many soap makers are becoming more mindful about the oils that they use in their products. For instance, the production of palm oil has been connected to the destruction of forests, the loss of biodiversity, and the relocation of indigenous tribes. Consequently, some soap manufacturers opt to either avoid palm oil entirely or acquire palm oil that has been produced in a manner that is environmentally responsible and has been verified by groups such as the Roundtable on Sustainable Palm Oil (RSPO).

Additionally, the ethical source of additional oils, such as shea butter and cocoa butter, is a concern for a great number of soap makers. When these components are purchased from fair trade or cooperatively owned suppliers, it can make a major difference in the lives of the farmers and workers who are involved in the production process. These ingredients are frequently produced in places where labor practices may be exploitative. Soap manufacturers who place a high priority on ethical and sustainable sourcing frequently showcase these values as part of their brand identity. This is done in order to attract customers who are looking for products that are in line with their own personal beliefs and principles.

One further thing to take into account when selecting oils for soapmaking is the possibility of allergies. Certain oils, particularly nut oils such as almond oil, macadamia oil, or walnut oil, have the potential to trigger allergic reactions in those who are extremely sensitive. When designing their recipes, soap makers should be conscious of the potential allergies that may be present in their products, particularly if they are making soap for sale or for large groups of people to use. Giving customers the opportunity to choose from a variety of hypoallergenic or nut-free soaps will help ensure that their products are available to the greatest number of individuals.

In addition to the fundamental oils that are utilized in the production of soap, numerous soap makers additionally incorporate luxury oils and additives into their products in order to improve the quality of their soaps. For instance, rosehip oil, which is abundant in vitamins and vital fatty acids, is frequently included in soaps that are designed for advanced age or skin that has been injured. Argan oil, which is particularly well-known for the high levels of antioxidants and fatty acids that it contains, is yet another popular luxury oil that can impart a smooth texture and conditioning benefits to soap. Due to the high cost of these specialized oils, they are normally only used in restricted quantities, yet they have the ability to transform a straightforward bar of soap into a very luxury product.

After the initial saponification process, soap makers have the ability to include more oils into their soap through the use of a procedure known as super fatting. After the soap has been combined and emulsified, soap makers can create bars that are more nutritious and hydrating by adding additional oils or butter to the mixture. The super fatting oils are allowed to remain in the soap without being completely saponified, which affords the skin the opportunity to absorb the beneficial characteristics of the oils. Jojoba oil, avocado oil, and shea butter are all examples of oils that are frequently used for super fatting. These oils all contribute to the creation of a luxurious and hydrating soap.

When selecting oils for soapmaking, it is essential to keep in mind the end goal of the soap that will be produced. It is possible that a soap designed for facial cleansing would prioritize oils that are gentle and conditioning, such as olive oil and avocado oil. On the other hand, a soap designed for use in the shower might benefit from the cleansing power of coconut oil and the hardness of palm oil or cocoa butter by utilizing these oils. Therefore, soap makers have the ability to experiment with various combinations of oils in order to discover the ideal balance for their requirements, regardless of whether they are making soap for their own personal use, as gifts, or for sale.

In conclusion, selecting the appropriate oils for soapmaking is a complicated and subtle process that requires striking a balance between the characteristics of various oils in order to accomplish the desired outcomes. Each individual component of the soap, ranging from base oils such as olive, coconut, and palm oil to specialized oils such as shea butter and avocado oil, contributes distinctive attributes to the finished product. These features include the soap's hardness, lather, conditioning properties, and overall atmosphere. In addition, soap makers are obligated to take into account the ethical and environmental repercussions of their decisions, as well as the possibility of allergens and the ultimate use of the soap. It is possible for soap makers to create beautiful, high-quality soaps that are tailored to their individual requirements and reflect their own beliefs, provided they have a thorough understanding of the qualities of various oils and how they interact with one another.

Fragrances and Essential Oils

The use of essential oils and fragrances is a vital part of the art of soapmaking. These components are responsible for elevating even the most basic bar of soap into a sensory experience. Despite the fact that the fundamental purpose of soap is to cleanse the skin, the addition of fragrance raises it to a higher level, turning the mundane routine of washing into an activity that is more joyful, more personal, and more therapeutic. When it comes to soapmaking, many soap makers believe that picking the appropriate fragrance or essential oil is equally as crucial as selecting the oils and additives that will decide the texture and conditioning capabilities of the soap products. A perfume that is well-selected has the ability to inspire a specific mood, encourage relaxation, or energize the senses. The sense of smell is powerful and closely tied to memory, emotion, and even well-being.

Artificial fragrance oils and natural essential oils are the two primary types of fragrances that are utilized in the soapmaking process. The decision between them is frequently determined by the objectives of the soap maker, the preferences of the end user, and factors like cost, longevity, and the possibility of skin irritation. Each of these soaps possesses its own unique set of traits, advantages, and limits. While essential oils give natural, plant-based aromas that frequently come with medicinal advantages due to their concentrated botanical qualities, synthetic fragrance oils offer a greater range of scent possibilities and are generally more economical. Synthetic fragrance oils also offer a wider range of scent possibilities.

Synthetic fragrance oils are substances that are manufactured in a laboratory with the purpose of imitating natural fragrances or producing wholly new aromas that may not be present in nature. Having access to such a wide range of fragrances is one of the many benefits that come with using synthetic fragrance oils. The aromas that soap makers can pick from include those that imitate the aroma of certain flowers, fruits, and spices, as well as some that are more abstract in nature, such as "ocean breeze" or "fresh linen." When it comes to soapmaking, having such a wide variety of possibilities enables more room for creativity and customization. Additionally, fragrance oils are typically more economical than essential oils, which makes them a cost-effective choice for soap makers who create soap in greater amounts or who wish to experiment with new scent combinations. Fragrance oils fall into the category of essential oils.

When it comes to soapmaking, fragrance oils are generally more stable than essential oils, which can occasionally lose their potency or change character throughout the saponification process. Fragrance oils, on the other hand, are more stable. Since fragrance oils are the result of chemical engineering, they are meant to be able to endure the high pH environment that is present during the soapmaking process. This means that the final scent in the soap is more likely to be identical to the fragrance oil that was used in the first place. Because of their dependability, fragrance oils are a popular choice among soap makers who want to ensure that their goods are consistent, particularly if they are manufacturing soap for the purpose of selling it.

There are, however, some downsides associated with synthetic scent oils. On account of the fact that they are manufactured in a laboratory, they do not provide the same natural advantages as essential oils. When it comes to soap makers and consumers who place high importance on the utilization of natural components, synthetic fragrance oils might not be compatible with their beliefs. Additionally, several fragrance oils have the potential to irritate the skin, particularly in people who have very sensitive skin or who suffer from allergies. When making soap, it is important to do thorough tests on fragrance oils to verify that they are safe for use on the skin. Additionally, soap makers should avoid using oils that include potentially hazardous chemicals such as phthalates, which are sometimes used to create fragrances that last longer.

However, essential oils are obtained from natural plant materials using methods such as steam distillation or cold pressing. These processes are used to extract essential oils. These essential oils are able to capture the essence of the plant from which they originate, carrying not only the aroma of the plant but also a concentrated form of its beneficial benefits. Essential oils have been utilized for their medicinal capabilities for thousands of years in a variety of civilizations. In addition to its aroma, many soap makers opt to include essential oils because of the natural and holistic benefits that they offer.

Anti-inflammatory, antibacterial, antiviral, and mood-enhancing benefits are just some of the properties that may be found in essential oils. Each essential oil has its own distinct profile of properties. Lavender essential oil, for instance, is well-known for its calming and relaxing effects, which is why it is a popular choice for soaps that are designed to encourage rest and relaxation. On the other hand, tea tree oil is well regarded for its antibacterial and antifungal characteristics, which makes it an excellent ingredient for soaps that are formulated for oily or acne-prone skin care products. Citrus oils, such as lemon or orange, are frequently utilized due to the fact that they possess natural cleansing characteristics in addition to having fragrances that are uplifting and stimulating.

Using essential oils in soapmaking has a number of advantages, one of which is that they come from natural sources. Essential oils provide a means by which natural aromas can be included in products, which is beneficial for customers who are searching for soap that does not contain any synthetic chemicals or artificial substances. The use of essential oils in high-end or handmade soaps is a popular choice because of the cachet that they carry. Essential oils are frequently connected with luxury and well-being, which makes them a popular choice.

On the other hand, utilizing essential oils in the soapmaking process poses its own unique set of difficulties. Essential oils are extremely concentrated, and if they are used improperly, they can cause irritation to the skin or even sensitization, which is a condition in which the skin grows increasingly sensitive to the oil over time. To ensure that their formulas adhere to the standards established by organizations such as the International Fragrance Association (IFRA), soap makers are required to conduct thorough research and accurately measure the quantities of essential oils that they intend to incorporate into their products. Some essential oils are only deemed safe when used in extremely low concentrations, while others may not be appropriate for products that are intended to be left on the skin, such as lotion, but are fine for products that are intended to be washed off, such as soap.

Essential oils provide a number of challenges, one of which is their volatility. There are a lot of essential oils that are sensitive to heat and light, which can cause them to lose their strength or alter aroma while they are being used in the soap formulation process. For example, the high pH environment that is present during the cold process of soapmaking has the potential to change the aroma of some essential oils, resulting in the final soap having a perfume that is distinct from what the soap maker had originally planned. Some soap makers prefer to add their essential oils at lower temperatures or utilize processes such as hot process soapmaking, which allows for the addition of essential oils after the soap has been saponified so it maintains more of the original scent. This is done in order to reduce the effects of this.

The medicinal and aromatic properties of essential oils make them a favorite among many soap makers, particularly those who specialize in developing natural, holistic, or aromatherapy-based products. Despite these challenges, essential oils are a favorite among soap makers. It is common practice for soap makers to select essential oils on the basis of their synergistic effects. By combining oils, soap makers are able to produce individualized fragrances that not only smell enticing but also provide particular advantages. It is possible, for instance, to make a soothing sleep soap by combining essential oils of lavender and chamomile. On the other hand, a mixture of eucalyptus and peppermint oils might be used to make a refreshing, energizing soap that is intended to wake up the senses.

After all is said and done, the decision between employing synthetic fragrance oils and essential oils is ultimately determined by the objectives and priorities of the soap maker. It is possible that some soap makers will opt to utilize solely essential oils in order to keep their product line entirely natural. On the other hand, other soap makers may prefer to integrate both fragrance and essential oils in order to make use of the distinct qualities that each possesses. In addition, there are hybrid solutions that can be utilized, such as fragrance oils that are partially derived from natural components but are strengthened with synthetic components in order to produce a scent that is more stable or that lasts for a longer period of time.

The concept of smell blending is something that soap makers take into consideration in addition to the use of essential oils and unique perfumes. In the same way that a chef will combine various spices and flavors in order to create a dish that is well-balanced, a soap maker can combine several oils in order to create a scent that is multifaceted and layered, and it will develop over time. For the purpose of developing a harmonious smell profile, it is essential to have a solid understanding of the fundamentals of fragrance blending, such as the top, middle, and base notes. The top notes are the smells that are not only the most delicate but also the most volatile. They are typically citrus or flowery in character, and they are the first aromas that are detected when the soap is smelled. Middle notes, also known as heart notes, are the central components of a fragrance and are typically more well-balanced and long-lasting. Base notes, on the other hand, are the most earthy and heaviest fragrances, and they are responsible for giving the fragrance depth and endurance.

An example of this would be a soap maker beginning with a bright and zesty top note like lemon or bergamot, then moving on to a floral center note such as geranium or lavender, and then concluding with a warm and earthy base note such as patchouli or cedarwood. Due to the fact that this results in a multifaceted scent that develops while the soap is used, it offers a more satisfying sensory experience than a fragrance that only has one note. Soap makers have the potential to produce really one-of-a-kind and customized soaps through the art of fragrance blending, which involves practice, experimentation, and a clear grasp of how different fragrances interact with one another.

The impact of scent on the performance of the soap is something that soap makers need to take into consideration in addition to their own personal preferences and creative ideas. A number of fragrance oils, particularly those that contain a significant amount of vanilla, have the potential to stain soap, causing it to turn brown or tan over the course of time. The reason for this is that the soap has a high concentration of vanillin, which is a component of vanilla extract and reacts with the alkaline environment of the soap. Despite the fact that this discoloration does not significantly impact the performance of the soap, it may be undesired if the soap maker is attempting to achieve a particular color palette or aesthetic appearance. There are several solutions to this problem, such as incorporating vanilla-stabilizing ingredients into the soap or accepting the natural color variations as an integral part of the soap's personality.

In a similar manner, many essential oils have the ability to speed up the trace, which is the stage in the soapmaking process at which the oils and lye combination begins to thicken. Clove oil and cinnamon oil, for example, are known for their ability to cause soap to quickly get frothy, which makes it difficult to pour into molds and results in a finish that is less smooth. Soap makers have a responsibility to be aware of the ways in which various oils influence the saponification process and to adapt their methods accordingly. This may involve working more rapidly, employing lower temperatures, or altering the formula in order to slow down the trace.

In addition, the use of fragrances and essential oils in the soapmaking process enables the production of products that are specifically formulated to address particular skin ailments or kinds. By way of illustration, tea tree oil, lavender oil, and chamomile oil are well-known for their calming and curative qualities, and they are frequently utilized in soaps that are formulated for skin that is prone to acne or is sensitive. Individuals who suffer from eczema, psoriasis, or any other skin ailment can benefit greatly from the use of these essential oils because they have the ability to alleviate inflammation, soothe irritation, and speed up the healing process. Additionally, essential oils such as peppermint, eucalyptus, and rosemary are energizing and can be utilized in soaps that are marketed toward athletes or individuals who are looking for a refreshing and cooling effect after engaging in physical activity.

In addition to the physical advantages, the aromatherapy properties of essential oils have the potential to improve the emotional and psychological impact of the soap it contains. Certain aromas, such as lavender, chamomile, and sandalwood, are well-known for their ability to alleviate stress and promote relaxation. As a result, these aromas are perfect for inclusion in soaps that are designed to encourage relaxation and sleep. On the other side, citrus aromas such as lemon, orange, and grapefruit are uplifting and energizing, and they contribute to an improvement in mood as well as an increase in mentally clear thinking. These qualities can be utilized by soap makers in order to construct soaps that not only cleanse the body but also contribute to the emotional well-being and equilibrium of the consumer.

To summarize, fragrances and essential oils play an important part in the process of creating soap. Not only do they contribute to the pleasant odors that make soap a pleasure to use, but they also have the potential to provide therapeutic advantages. The priorities of the soap maker should be taken into consideration when making the decision between using synthetic fragrance oils or natural essential oils. All of these options come with their own unique set of benefits and difficulties. Soap makers have access to an extraordinary variety of fragrances, which they can use for a variety of purposes, like encouraging creativity and reducing costs through the use of fragrance oils or exploring the natural and holistic benefits of essential oils. Soap makers are able to create luxurious, high-quality soaps that transform mundane activities into experiences of beauty, well-being, and self-care by first gaining a grasp of the qualities of various oils, then experimenting with smell blending, and finally taking into consideration the effects that their decisions have on both the body and the mind.

Color and Texture Additives

Making soap is an art form that involves more than just the creation of smells and cleansing properties; it also entails the creation of items that are aesthetically pleasing and that thrill the senses. Additives that impart color and texture are essential components in the process of elevating ordinary soap to the level of a work of art. Infusing their compositions with brilliant colors and one-of-a-kind tactile sensations that enrich the entire experience for the user is something that soap maker are able to do through the utilization of these additions. The possibilities for customization are virtually limitless, and they range from natural clays and botanicals to synthetic colorants and exfoliants. The choice of color and texture additives not only enables aesthetic expression but also has the potential to communicate the specific function of soap, the substances it contains, or the audience it is intended for. For people who are interested in making soaps for personal use, as gifts, or for sale, these components are essential, particularly in situations where the visual appeal of the soap is a significant influence in attracting clients.

Natural and synthetic color additives are two major categories that can be used to classify color additives. Each of these categories has its own set of advantages and disadvantages. Natural colorants, which are generated from plant-based materials, clays, and minerals, are frequently selected by soap maker who place an emphasis on the utilization of environmentally friendly, sustainable, or organic components. Among the most widely used natural colorants are alkanet root, which imparts a purple hue; turmeric, which imparts yellow and orange hues; and spirulina, which imparts green hues. Customers who are sensitive to synthetic dyes and those who are looking for products that do not include any chemicals are likely to be interested in these natural solutions. Additionally, natural colorants frequently offer other advantages in addition to the coloring capabilities they possess. For instance, clays such as French green clay or bentonite clay are not only used to impart color but they are also used to pull impurities from the skin. Because of this, clays found in facial soaps or detoxifying bars are appropriate for usage in these products.

However, natural colorants might be problematic in certain situations, notably when it comes to the production of cold-process soap. The high pH of cold process soap can lead natural colorants to react in an unpredictable manner, which might result in colors that fade or transform into shades that were not intended during the saponification process. As an illustration, certain plant-based colorants that are vivid while they are in oil form can turn out to be subdued or brown when they are used in soap. In addition, natural colorants could not generate colors that are as vibrant or vivid as those produced by synthetic dyes. This can be a hindrance for soap maker who are looking for specific colors that are vivid. Particularly when using botanical ingredients, which might vary in potency from harvest to harvest, the variety in color results can also make it difficult to generate uniform batches. This is especially true when utilizing botanical additives.

The use of synthetic colorants, on the other hand, provides greater control and reliability in terms of the color output. These colorants, which include micas, oxides, and FD&C (Food, Drug, and Cosmetic) dyes, are created in order to provide tints that are consistent and bright between batches. Micas, which are made from natural minerals and coated with colorants, are particularly popular in the soapmaking industry because of their ability to impart sparkly, iridescent colors that are noticeable in the final product. Micas are generated from natural minerals. Micas are available in a broad variety of hues, ranging from delicate pastels to vibrant jewel tones, and they are stable in both the cold process and melt-and-pour soapmaking procedures. Micas can be found in several colors. Since oxides are stable and have the potential to produce colors that are rich and opaque, they are also widely employed in the production of soap. Examples of oxides are titanium dioxide and iron oxide.

Because they are water-soluble, synthetic dyes such as FD&C colorants are frequently utilized in the production of transparent soaps or melt-and-pour bases in order to produce colors that are bright and translucent. As a result of their consistency and ease of application, these dyes are an excellent choice for soap maker who are looking to produce colorful and consistent products without the uncertainty that comes with using natural colorants. Additionally, synthetic colorants typically offer a more strong color saturation, which enables soap maker to use a smaller quantity of dye to produce the desired effect. This can be a cost-effective method for producing larger quantities of soap.

Some consumers are hesitant to use items that contain artificial colors, particularly those that are generated from petroleum or contain heavy metals. This is because synthetic colorants offer a number of benefits, but some consumers are suspicious of utilizing these products. For this reason, soap maker who market their goods as all-natural, organic, or environmentally friendly may decide to forego synthetic dyes in favor of more natural solutions despite the obstacles that synthetic dyes provide.

There is a wide range of components that may be put into soap in order to provide a number of various tactile experiences. All of these components can be used to give texture to soap. Exfoliants, for example, are a common choice among soap maker who wish to create scrubbing bars that assist in the removal of dead skin cells and improve circulation at the same time. In the process of manufacturing soap, exfoliants such as ground oats, coffee grounds, sugar, sea salt, and seeds or nuts that have been finely powdered are frequently used. Some of these additives provide a gentle buffing action, such as colloidal oats, while others provide a more forceful scouring power, such as sea salt or coffee grounds. Each of these additives delivers a distinct level of exfoliation.

In many cases, the choice of exfoliant is determined by the purpose for which the soap will be used. For instance, a facial soap may require the use of a moderate exfoliant such as ground oats or jojoba beads. These exfoliants offer a gentle exfoliation that does not irritate the sensitive skin of the face. While body soaps are able to handle more robust exfoliants such as sea salt, pumice, or coffee grounds, these exfoliants assist in smoothing rough skin and eliminate impurities from the skin. Some soap maker even develop dual-texture soaps by including exfoliants on one side of the bar and leaving the other side of the bar smooth for parts of the body that are more susceptible to the effects of the lotion.

It is also possible to employ botanical additives to impart color and texture to soap. Some examples of botanical additives are dried flowers, herbs, and seeds. It is standard practice to sprinkle dried lavender buds, rose petals, calendula petals, and chamomile flowers on top of soap bars or embed them within the soap itself in order to produce an appearance that is both artistic and luxurious. Not only do these botanicals improve the appeal of the soap from a visual standpoint, but they also have the potential to contribute to the whole sensory experience. This is especially true when combined with essential oils or smells that complement one another. As an illustration, a soap that is perfumed with lavender and has dried lavender buds strewn on top has both visual and olfactory appeal, which results in a product that is coherent and agreeable to the senses.

Nevertheless, the utilization of botanicals in the production of soap can present its own unique set of difficulties. There is a possibility that certain dried flowers and herbs can get discolored or dark during the process of creating soap, particularly in cold process soap. The visual appeal of the soap may suffer as a result of this if the soap maker is not well prepared for the changes that are occurring. Furthermore, larger botanicals, such as full flower heads or large herb sprigs, may not dissolve during usage and may produce a rough or scratchy feel, which may be undesirable for some users. This includes the possibility that the texture will be unpleasant. It is common practice for soap maker to grind botanicals into finer paper or to use them sparingly as a decorative feature on the surface of the soap rather than throughout the entire bar. This is done in order to mitigate the problems that have been described.

Ingredients that are hydrating or conditioning can also be considered texture additives since they improve the way the soap feels when it is applied to the skin. It is common practice to incorporate butter like shea butter, cocoa butter, and mango butter into soap formulas due to the fact that these butter have a luxurious, creamy consistency and are known to be hydrating. This butter contributes to the formation of a luscious and silky lather that infuses the skin with a sense of softness and nourishment. Similarly, honey, aloe vera, and silk fibers are some of the components that can be added to soap in order to improve its moisturizing properties and produce an experience that is more luxurious and reminiscent of a traditional spa.

Additionally, clays are a common type of texture addition used in soapmaking. It is usual practice to use bentonite, kaolin, and French green clay in soap in order to impart more beneficial properties to the skin while also imparting a silky and smooth texture. Clays are a popular choice for facial soaps, and soaps made for oily or acne-prone skin because of their ability to help absorb excess oils. They also contribute to the soap's creamy lather, which contributes to an overall improvement in the sensory experience. Clays, in addition to the textural qualities they offer, frequently produce hues that are natural and subdued, which makes them a flexible additive that may be used for both form and function.

Soap's visual and tactile appeal is not only vital for personal usage, but it also plays a key role in the commercial market. This is because soap is sold to consumers. The inclusion of color and texture additives can help differentiate a soap from its competitors since consumers are frequently drawn to soaps that have a rich appearance and feel while also being aesthetically pleasing. Handmade soap maker, in particular, frequently employ one-of-a-kind color and texture combinations as a means of distinguishing their products from those that are widely produced in vast quantities. A straightforward bar of soap can be transformed into a work of practical art by the application of vivid colors, complicated swirls, and unique textures. This has the potential to make the bar of soap an appealing choice for gift-giving or as a treat for oneself.

Techniques that include swirling, for example, have become increasingly popular as a means of incorporating color into handcrafted soap. In order to create elaborate, marbled patterns in the finished soap, swirling entails piling or pouring several colors of soap batter in such a way that they work together to form the design. There are many various swirling effects that may be created by soap maker using a variety of implements, such as chopsticks, spoons, or spatulas. These swirling effects range from subtle swaths of color to bold and dramatic patterns. Creating visually striking soaps can be accomplished through the use of swirling, which is a versatile technique that can be used in both melt-and-pour soapmaking and cold-process soapmaking.

Layering is yet another method that can be utilized to produce soaps that are visually appealing. It is possible for soap maker to produce stripes, gradients, or even geometric patterns in the completed bar by pouring different colors of soap batter in successive layers. This method is frequently utilized in the production of themed soaps, such as those with holiday or seasonal motifs, or in order to highlight the many components that comprise a dish of soap. For instance, a soap that is created with activated charcoal and peppermint essential oil might have a layered design that is black and white. This would be done in order to visually symbolize the cleansing characteristics of the charcoal and the invigorating aroma of the peppermint.

There are some soap makers that explore more advanced color processes, such as embedding or sculpting, in addition to the more classic techniques of swirling and layering. Before the soap mixture solidifies, the process of embedding entails inserting pre-made soap shapes or items into the soap batter. Some examples of these include soap curls, stars, and hearts. In the completed bar of soap, this results in a three-dimensional impression, with the embedded forms becoming a component of the bar itself. By shaping the soap batter into various shapes or textures, such as creating peaks or waves on the surface of the soap, sculpting is a technique that can be used to create artwork. The use of these techniques calls for a high level of ability and precision, but they have the potential to produce soaps that are really artistic and one-of-a-kind, making them stand out in the market.

Additionally, the selection of color and texture additions has repercussions for the branding and marketing of the product. It is common practice for soap maker who sell their products to employ color and texture in order to establish a consistent brand identity. For instance, a soap maker that specializes in natural and organic products can decide to utilize solely earth-toned colorants, such as clays and botanicals, in order to reflect the natural components that are used in their soaps. Alternatively, a soap maker that portrays their products as fun and whimsical can employ bright, vibrant colors and playful textures, such as glitter or confetti soap embeds, in order to appeal to a younger audience. This would be done in order to attract a younger audience.

Generally speaking, color and texture additions are instruments that are indispensable to the arsenal of a soap maker. In addition to enriching the sensory experience of using soap, they make it possible for individuals to express themselves creatively and personally. In order to create beautiful and sumptuous soaps, soap maker have a broad variety of alternatives available to them. These possibilities include the use of natural colorants, which are more environmentally friendly, as well as synthetic dyes, which produce results that are brilliant and consistent. By offering a tactile experience that compliments the soap's visual beauty, texture additives, which can range from exfoliants to moisturizing butter, further increase the appeal of the soap. Experimentation, practice, and a comprehensive understanding of the components and methods involved in soapmaking are two of the most important factors that contribute to success in the soapmaking process. In order to enhance their craft and create genuinely extraordinary goods that please the senses and nourish the skin, soap maker can elevate their art by carefully selecting and thoughtfully applying color and texture additives.

CHAPTER III

Soapmaking Techniques

Cold Process Soap

In the world of soapmaking, cold-process soapmaking is considered to be one of the most traditional and renowned ways. This method provides artists with the opportunity to create high-quality soaps that can be customized from the ground up. The transformation of fats or oils, water, and lye into a solid bar of soap is accomplished through the use of a chemical reaction known as saponification, which has been utilized for centuries. Cold-process soapmaking, in contrast to other processes such as melt-and-pour or hot-process soapmaking, enables the maker to exert a greater degree of control over the soap's components, including its texture, aroma, and aesthetic design. In addition to this, it gives soap maker the chance to experiment with a wide variety of additions, such as essential oils, botanicals, and natural colorants. Nevertheless, in order to guarantee that the finished product is not only safe but also useful and visually beautiful, cold-process soapmaking necessitates a profound comprehension of the chemistry that underlies the soapmaking process, in addition to patience and precision.

The cold process method begins with the mixing of oils and a lye solution, which is produced by dissolving sodium hydroxide, more frequently referred to as lye, in water. This is the fundamental principle behind the cold process method. The process of saponification is then initiated by gently incorporating this lye solution into the oils. During the process of saponification, the triglycerides that are present in the oils undergo a chemical reaction that results in the formation of soap by converting them into glycerin and fatty acid salts. Cold process soap is distinguished by the fact that the heat necessary for saponification is produced by the chemical reaction itself, as opposed to being provided externally. This is one of the defining properties of cold-process soap. Because of this, the soap is able to cure gradually over a period of time, which contributes to its natural moisturizing characteristics, gentleness, and long-lasting durability.

One of the most significant advantages of creating soap using the cold process is the extensive range of oils that may be utilized to produce soap of varying grades thanks to the cold process. Each oil brings its own set of distinctive qualities to the finished product of the mixture. One example is olive oil, which is frequently used because of its hydrating and mild properties, making it an excellent choice for skin that is sensitive. On the other hand, coconut oil produces a bar that is firm, clean and has a generous amount of foam. It is common practice to use palm oil because of its capacity to produce a bar that is solid and long-lasting, but castor oil is highly prized for its capacity to generate a lather that is creamy and stable. In order to achieve the necessary level of hardness, cleansing ability, and moisturizing properties in the finished soap, soap maker frequently construct bespoke combinations of oils. This allows them to achieve the desired balance of these features.

The careful selection of oils also makes it possible to incorporate specialized components, such as butter and unusual oils, into the recipe. In cold-process soapmaking, shea butter, cocoa butter, and mango butter are common additions since they contribute to the moisturizing properties of the soap as well as its rich texture. The fact that these butters are abundant in vitamins and fatty acids makes them an excellent choice for enhancing the overall texture of the soap as well as providing nourishment to the skin. In a similar vein, oils such as jojoba oil, argan oil, and avocado oil are frequently utilized due to the wonderful effects they have on the skin. These oils offer intense hydration and promote the skin's suppleness respectively. In addition to improving the efficacy of the soap, the use of these specialized oils and butter contributes to the product's overall appeal as a luxury item.

One of the most important aspects that distinguishes cold-process soapmaking from other processes is the ability to exercise complete control over the formulation of the soap used in the process. Due to the fact that cold-process soap is manufactured from scratch, soap maker have full control over the components that are used in the production of their liquid soap. Because this makes it possible to employ natural, organic, or environmentally friendly components, cold-process soap is an appealing choice for individuals who place a high priority on both the health of their skin and the preservation of the environment. Several manufacturers of cold-process soaps make the decision to steer clear of synthetic ingredients and instead use natural colorants, perfumes, and preservatives in their products. Through this process, a product is created that is typically less abrasive on the skin and does not contain any of the harsh chemicals that are typically found in commercial soaps.

There is also the possibility of incorporating a wide range of additives into cold-process soap, such as essential oils, clays, botanicals, and exfoliants. This is yet another significant advantage of cold-process soap. It is possible for soap maker to create customized soaps that are tailored to specific skin types, requirements, or preferences by using these additions. To give just one example, essential oils are typically included due to the fragrant and therapeutic capabilities that they possess. One of the most common choices for cold-process soap is a lavender essential oil, which is well-known for its calming and soothing qualities. Tea tree oil, on the other hand, is frequently incorporated due to the antibacterial and anti-inflammatory properties it possesses. It is possible for soap maker to manufacture soaps that not only wash the skin but also provide aromatherapy advantages, hence enriching the overall experience of the user. This is made possible by the utilization of essential oils.

In addition, clays and botanicals are frequently utilized in cold-process soap in order to impart color, texture, and potential benefits to the skin. Clays such as French green clay, bentonite clay, and kaolin clay are widely used as additives because of their capacity to absorb impurities and give a texture that is smooth and velvety. Botanicals, which include dried flowers, herbs, and seeds, can be utilized in the production of soaps that are not only visually appealing but also include qualities that are exfoliating or calming. For example, dried lavender buds, rose petals, or calendula petals are frequently placed on top of soap or embedded within the bar as a beautiful touch. Other examples are calendula petals and rose petals. Poppy seeds, powdered oats, and coffee grounds are all examples of ingredients that can be included for their exfoliating properties. These ingredients help to remove dead skin cells and strengthen circulation.

When producing soap using the cold process, one of the most creative parts is the opportunity to construct beautiful patterns and textures inside the soap itself. In order to create swirls, layers, or embeds inside the soap, soap maker have a variety of ways at their disposal. This is due to the fact that the soap batter remains fluid for a period of time before it begins to firm. The process of swirling involves putting soap batter of varying colors into the mold and then manipulating implements such as chopsticks or spoons to create marbled patterns throughout the soap. The use of this method is widespread since it allows for the production of soaps that are not only practical but also visually appealing and considered to be works of art. Creating striped or ombré designs can be accomplished through the process of layering, which involves pouring numerous layers of soap batter of varying colors in successive order. With the intention of producing a three-dimensional look, some soap maker even incorporate pre-made soap shapes into the soap mix. These shapes may include stars, hearts, or curls.

When compared to other processes, cold-process soapmaking is characterized by a higher level of skill and attention to detail despite the fact that it offers a multitude of benefits. Because lye is a caustic material, soap maker are required to take safety precautions when working with it. These precautions include wearing gloves and goggles and working in an area that has adequate ventilation. Moreover, it is of the utmost importance to correctly measure the components, as soap that has either an excessive amount of lye or an insufficient amount of it might be either too harsh or too soft. It is necessary to mix the soap batter until it reaches the desired consistency, which is referred to as "trace," which indicates that the oils and lye have both completely emulsified. Due to the fact that under-mixing can result in soap that separates, and over-mixing can result in soap that hardens too soon, making it difficult to pour into the mold, it is essential to achieve the appropriate trace.

The process of curing the soap begins once it has been put into the mold, and it can take many weeks for the process to be finished. Over the course of this period, the soap will continue to saponify and harden, and any excess water will evaporate off the bar and disappear. If the soap is left to cure for a longer period of time, it will become more durable and more long-lasting. Although the normal curing time for cold-process soap is between four and six weeks, some soap maker prefer to let their soap cure for even longer in order to attain the highest possible level of hardness and lather performance.

Making soap using the cold method has a number of obstacles, one of which is the possibility of the end product being unpredictable. This is especially true when working with natural colorants or specific ingredients. During the curing process, for instance, certain natural colorants may lose their intensity or transform into unexpected hues. Additionally, certain perfumes may lose their potency or alter in character throughout the course of the curing process. In addition, the high pH of cold-process soap might cause certain botanicals to have a brownish or discolored appearance. In order to get the desired results, soap maker need to experiment with various combinations of ingredients and procedures. They frequently keep thorough records of their formulations in order to guarantee consistency in subsequent batches.

Many soap maker consider cold-process soapmaking to be a gratifying and satisfying craft despite the difficulties that are involved in the process. When compared to other ways of soapmaking, the ability to make a product from scratch using natural and high-quality ingredients enables a level of creativity and personalization that is difficult to accomplish with other methods. Cold-process soap is frequently considered to be a premium product due to the fact that it is recognized for its sensuous feel, gentle washing properties, and handmade manufacturing quality. In addition to being used for personal enjoyment, as a gift, or for sale, cold process soap offers a one-of-a-kind combination of art and science, which opens up a world of possibilities for individuals who are enthusiastic about the process of making beautiful handmade items.

In addition to its aesthetic and sensual appeal, cold-process soap is particularly valued for the positive effects It has on the environment. Using sustainable and ethically obtained ingredients is a priority for many soap maker. Some examples of these components are organic oils and butter, palm oil that comes from verified sustainable sources, and so on. Cold-process soap is a more environmentally friendly alternative to mass-produced commercial soaps, which are frequently prepared with materials derived from petroleum and packed in plastic. Cold-process soap is made by eliminating the use of synthetic detergents, preservatives, and harsh chemicals. Additionally, the production of cold-process soap results in a small amount of waste, particularly when molds and tools that can be reused are utilized. In addition, many soap maker reduce waste by reusing residual soap scraps, making soap balls or embeds from leftover soap batter, or a combination of these two methods.

In recent years, there has been a rise in the demand for natural, handmade, and artisanal products, which has contributed to the popularity of cold-process soapmaking. In order to cater to customers who are looking for high-quality, one-of-a-kind soaps that reflect their values and preferences, soap maker frequently offer their products at farmers' markets, artisan fairs, and online platforms. In addition to being a friendly and collaborative space, the community of handmade soap maker is also a place where soap maker share advice, recipes, and skills with one another through online forums, social media groups, and workshops. For individuals who are passionate about soapmaking, cold process soapmaking is a craft that is both deeply rewarding and engaging because of the sense of community that is involved in the process, as well as the creative and technical components of soapmaking.

In conclusion, cold-process soapmaking is a time-honored method that provides an infinite number of opportunities for creativity, customization, and self-expression. The cold process soapmaking process is both an art form and a science. From the meticulous selection of oils and additives to the elaborate design processes used to produce patterns and textures, cold-process soapmaking is a multifaceted process. Despite the fact that the procedure calls for patience, precision, and an in-depth comprehension of the chemistry involved, the end product is a rich soap of superior quality that is kind to the skin and is also kind to the environment.

Melt and Pour Method

One of the most common and easily available methods for producing handmade soap is the melt-and-pour method. This method is particularly useful for novices or individuals who are searching for a more straightforward and expedient approach to soapmaking. The melt-and-pour technique of soapmaking eliminates the need to handle lye directly, in contrast to the cold process method of soapmaking, which requires working with lye and oils from scratch. Instead, the melt-and-pour method employs a pre-made soap base that has already been saponified. Because of this, it is a more user-friendly solution because it eliminates some of the hazards and complications that are connected with the traditional method of soap fabrication. When using the melt-and-pour method, the soap is ready to use as soon as it solidifies in the mold, which normally takes only a few hours. This makes the melt-and-pour method a speedier method because it does not require a lengthy curing time span. As a result of this simplicity, as well as the versatility it provides in terms of personalization, the melt-and-pour method has become a favorite among hobbyists, crafters, and even expert soap maker who wish to create decorative or utilitarian soaps in a short amount of time.

The pre-made soap base is the fundamental component of the melt-and-pour soapmaking process. This base is offered in a wide range of formulations to cater to a variety of preferences and various requirements. The same oils, water, and lye that are used to make traditional soap are also used to make these bases. However, in addition to these ingredients, they also include additions such as glycerin and sorbitol, which are responsible for their characteristic transparency and pliability. Due to the fact that glycerin is a humectant, which means that it draws moisture to the skin, soap bases that contain glycerin are exceptionally delicate and hydrating substances. Shea butter, cocoa butter, and goat's milk are some of the additional components that are used in some soap bases. These compounds contribute even more nourishing characteristics to the finished soap. The vast selection of bases that are available gives soap maker the ability to select one that corresponds with the conclusion that they want to achieve, whether that be a soap that is transparent and translucent, a bar that is opaque and creamy, or one that is enhanced with certain moisturizing or conditioning ingredients.

For the purpose of initiating the melt-and-pour process, the soap base is initially sliced into manageable bits, and then it is melted down until it reaches a liquid state. In accordance with one's individual preferences, this can be accomplished either in a microwave or by using a double boiler. In order to prevent the soap from becoming overly thick, forming bubbles, or losing its smooth texture, it is essential to melt the base in a gentle manner while avoiding overheating itself. The foundation, once it has been melted, transforms into a blank canvas that can be individualized with a broad variety of additions, including perfumes, colorants, exfoliants, and other components. Because the base has already been saponified, the soap maker is able to concentrate solely on the cosmetic and functional features of the soap without having to worry about the chemical reaction that occurs between the oils and the lye.

In the process of creating melt & pour soap, the fragrance is typically one of the most widely used additions. The base can be melted, and then essential oils or fragrance oils can be added to it in order to produce a soap that has a pleasing aroma. Essential oils are obtained from natural plant sources and offer not only fragrant benefits but also medicinal capabilities. Essential oils are useful for a variety of purposes. One example is the peaceful and soothing properties of lavender, while peppermint can deliver a refreshing and energizing experience. Lavender is known for its calming and soothing effects. Additionally, essential oils, which can lose their potency over time or react in an unpredictable manner with other components, are not as stable in soap as fragrance oils, which are synthetically generated to replicate natural fragrances. Fragrance oils give a greater choice of fragrance alternatives and can occasionally be more stable in soap than essential oils. It is common practice for soap maker to experiment with various combinations of essential and fragrance oils in order to develop trademark fragrances or soaps that are suited to particular states of mind, events, or skin types.

Melt-and-pour soap can also be customized with colorants, which is another popular method. Clays, herbs, and botanicals are examples of natural colorants that are available, but synthetic dyes and pigments are also available. There is a wide variety of possibilities available. Natural colorants, such as spirulina powder, turmeric powder, or beetroot powder, are preferred by individuals who favor an all-natural approach. Synthetic dyes, such as FD&C colorants or micas, provide colors that are brilliant and uniform, and they are less prone to fade over time. As a result of the clear and translucent quality of many melt-and-pour bases, it is possible to create spectacular effects with color, such as layered designs, swirls, or embeds. For instance, soap maker might create a gradient effect by pouring different colored layers of soap into the bar. Alternatively, they can insert smaller soap forms or items into the bar for a whimsical and colorful touch. Because of the versatility of melt-and-pour soapmaking, the only real limitation is the imagination of the person making the soap.

Melt & pour soap can be improved with a variety of ingredients that offer skin benefits or unique textures in addition to the scent and color that are usually included in the formulation. In order to provide a mild scouring action, exfoliants like ground oats, coffee grounds, or pumice can be added to the soap. This will assist in the removal of dead skin cells and will also aid in stimulating circulation. Honey, aloe vera, and botanical extracts are examples of nourishing ingredients that soap maker can incorporate into their products to create a more luxurious feel. These substances are known for their ability to moisturize, soothe, or heal the skin. Other popular additives include dried flowers, herbs, or seeds. These ingredients not only give aesthetic value to the product, but they also have the potential to provide extra advantages to the skin, such as reducing inflammation or functioning as a mild astringent ingredient.

Intricate designs and shapes that would be difficult to achieve with other ways of soapmaking can be created with melt-and-pour soapmaking, which is one of the distinctive features of this method of making soap. This allows soap maker to pour the soap base into molds of varying shapes and sizes, including highly detailed silicone molds that produce soaps in the shape of flowers, animals, or other figures. This is made possible by the fact that the soap base remains liquid for a length of time before it begins to harden when it is poured into molds. In addition, soap maker have the ability to produce striped or ombré effects by layering different colors of soap, or they can create a marbled appearance by swirling multiple colors together. Melt-and-pour soapmaking is a popular choice for manufacturing gifts, party favors, or ornamental soaps since it allows for infinite versatility in terms of design and presentation. This is because the soap base can be readily manipulated, which allows for endless innovation.

Melt-and-pour soapmaking is advantageous for a number of reasons, including the fact that the technique is both quick and convenient. There is no need for a curing time, which is required in cold-process soapmaking because the soap base has already been saponified. This eliminates the requirement for the curing period. The soap will normally solidify within a few hours after it has been put into the mold, at which point it will be ready for use. Because of this, it is an excellent choice for individuals who are interested in making soap in a short amount of time or who may not have the time or space to allow for lengthy curing times. Additionally, melt and pour soap is a procedure that produces a comparatively modest amount of mess because it does not require the handling of raw lye or the cleanup that is associated with oils and lye residue.

The production of soap using the melt-and-pour process has a number of advantages, but it also has significant drawbacks in comparison to other approaches. For example, because the soap base has already been manufactured, the soap maker has less control over the components that go into the soap as well as the qualities that it ultimately possesses. Because of this, it is conceivable that it will not be possible to get the same level of customization in terms of the soap's ability to cleanse, its lather, or its hardness as it would be possible to create with cold process or hot process procedures. In addition, melt-and-pour soap has a tendency to generate a soap that is softer and more prone to melting in humid settings. This is in contrast to cold process soap, which is often more durable and lasts longer due to the lengthier curing process.

In spite of these drawbacks, melt-and-pour soapmaking continues to be a well-liked and easily accessible alternative for soap maker of all experience levels. The process of making personalized soaps with a wide range of smells, colors, and designs may be accomplished in a way that is not only simple but also enjoyable. As a result of the straightforward nature of the procedure, it is an excellent option for individuals who are interested in beginning the process of soapmaking but do not possess the necessary specialized equipment or a comprehensive understanding of chemistry. At the same time, the vast selection of soap bases and additions that are available makes it possible for even experienced soap maker to experiment with new designs, methods, and components. This ensures that there is always something new to learn in the realm of melt-and-pour soapmaking.

Making soap with the melt-and-pour method provides potential for small-scale business endeavors as well as gift-giving, in addition to providing enjoyable experiences for the maker. Once they learn that their friends, family, or even local markets are interested in purchasing their creations, many soap maker begin their journey by manufacturing melt-and-pour soaps as a pastime. Melt and pour soaps are an appealing choice for individuals who are interested in selling homemade soaps or making personalized gifts for special occasions because of their ability to manufacture beautifully patterned and scented soaps in a short amount of time. It doesn't matter if you're making a batch of lavender-scented bars for holiday gifts, a set of heart-shaped soaps for wedding favor, or a custom soap for a boutique skincare line; melt and pour soapmaking offers the versatility and efficiency that are necessary to meet demand while still maintaining a high level of quality and craftsmanship.

It is possible to experiment and iterate fast when producing melt-and-pour soap, which is one of the reasons why this method is so popular. Due to the fact that the soap is ready to use quickly after it has hardened, soap maker are able to experiment with new smells, colorants, and additives without having to wait weeks for the soap to cure through the process. Rapid prototyping and experimentation are made possible as a result of this, which makes it simpler to create new recipes or improve upon those that already exist. In a very short amount of time, soap maker have the opportunity to experiment with various combinations of essential oils, experiment with techniques such as layering or swirling, and test the effects of various exfoliants and moisturizers, among other things. Melt-and-pour soapmaking is frequently seen as a creative outlet because it provides soap maker with the opportunity to express their individuality and artistry via the designs of their soaps. One of the reasons for this is the freedom to explore that is inherent in the process.

There are a lot of people who are interested in melt-and-pour soapmaking because it allows them to make soaps that are suitable for specific occasions or themes. As a result of the simplicity with which the soap base can be melted and poured into molds of varying shapes and sizes, it is usual practice for soap maker to create unique soaps for special occasions such as holidays or celebrations. For instance, soaps with a Halloween theme can have eerie shapes like pumpkins or ghosts, and they might be colored orange and black. On the other hand, soaps with a Christmas theme might have festive aromas like peppermint or cinnamon, and they might be shaped like snowflakes or candy canes. Because of its adaptability, melt-and-pour soap is a popular choice for the creation of colorful, beautiful soaps that are in line with particular occasions, holidays, or seasons. These soaps bring an additional layer of enjoyment to the experience for both the person who creates the soap and the person who receives it.

When it comes to the influence that soapmaking has on the environment, making soap using the melt-and-pour method can be a more environmentally responsible alternative to purchasing commercial soaps, which frequently contain synthetic components and are packed in plastic. There are a lot of melt-and-pour soap bases that are manufactured with natural materials, and some of them are even available in organic or sustainably derived versions. Furthermore, because soap maker have the ability to manage the additives that they incorporate into their products, it is feasible to manufacture soaps that are devoid of any potentially dangerous chemicals, artificial preservatives, or synthetic fragrances. In addition, the production of melt-and-pour soap results in a low amount of waste, particularly when molds and tools that are reusable are utilized. The remaining soap batter or soap scraps from trimming can be simply remelted and recycled into new bars, which will result in a reduction in the overall amount of waste.

Melt & pour soapmaking presents a reasonably low entrance barrier for individuals who are intrigued by the prospect of beginning a soapmaking business. Due to the fact that the process does not call for expensive equipment or substantial training, it is an approachable method for beginning the production of handcrafted soaps specifically for commercial sale. Soap maker are able to manufacture huge quantities of soap in a short period of time due to the fact that the soap is easy to make and does not require any curing time. This can be especially beneficial during busy times within the industry, such as during the holiday season. With melt-and-pour soap, soap maker are able to create a one-of-a-kind product line by experimenting with various combinations of aromas, colors, and designs. Melt-and-pour soap also lends itself nicely to branding and customization. Melt & pour soap can be an enticing product for clients who are looking for high-quality, handcrafted soaps that offer a personal touch. This is true whether the soap is sold at local craft fairs, farmer's markets, or online platforms.

To summarize, the melt-and-pour method of soapmaking offers a process that is not only easy to use but also adaptable and creative, allowing for the creation of beautiful soaps with the least work and maximum customization attainable. When soap maker make use of a pre-made soap foundation, they are able to concentrate on the artistic parts of the soapmaking process. They are able to experiment with a wide range of aromas, colors, and additives in order to create individualized soaps that are reflective of their individual preferences and characteristics. Because of its ease of use and convenience, the melt-and-pour method is an excellent option for novices, enthusiasts, and expert soap maker alike. It provides an infinite number of chances for creative expression and self-expression. A fun, gratifying, and practical approach to experiencing the art of soap creation is to make soap using the melt-and-pour method. This method can be used to make soap for personal use, as a gift, or for sale.

Advanced Designs: Swirls and Layers

When it comes to soapmaking, having a greater understanding of both the artistic and technical components of the craft is necessary in order to create complex designs such as swirls and layers. Because of the visual intricacy and elegance that they can provide to handmade soaps, swirls and layers are two of the most popular design techniques that are employed in the soapmaking industry. In order to generate one-of-a-kind and visually acceptable outcomes, each approach requires a mix of exact time, control over the texture of the soap, and careful manipulation of colors and smells. Despite the fact that the fundamental principles of soapmaking have not changed, the innovative techniques that are utilized to make swirls and layers add an element of creativity that takes the craft to a new level.

First and foremost, a strong foundation of soapmaking knowledge is required in order to begin the process of making swirling and layered soaps. As a result of the fact that it provides the soap maker with additional time to work with the soap batter before it hardens, the cold process method is the technique that is utilized the most frequently for the creation of complex soap designs. When manufacturing soap using the cold process, oils are mixed with a lye solution, and then the resulting combination is subjected to saponification in order to generate soap. It is essential to pay close attention to timing while using this approach, particularly when it comes to producing the desired consistency of the soap batter for swirls and layers. The creation of elaborate motifs is made more difficult when the soap thickens at an excessively rapid rate. On the other hand, if it continues to be too thin, the colors have the potential to bleed into each other, which will result in an appearance that is less clear.

Within the realm of soapmaking, the term "swirling" refers to the process of generating elaborate patterns by the manipulation of various colored soap batter. Soap maker are able to produce stunning, flowing designs using this process. These designs can range from tiny wisps to strong, dramatic patterns. In-the-pot swirl, drop swirl, hanger swirl, and Taiwan swirl are some of the different types of swirl techniques that soap maker might utilize, depending on the outcome they want to achieve. Other swirl techniques include the Taiwan swirl. It is necessary to have a certain level of control over the texture of the soap in order to use each technique, as well as a solid understanding of how the various colors will interact with one another after they are poured into the mold. The specific kind of swirl that is used will also have an effect on the overall appearance of the soap once it has been cut into bars.

When it comes to swirling techniques, the in-the-pot swirl is one of the easiest and most extensively utilized procedures. The process of creating an in-the-pot swirl involves soap maker preparing multiple amounts of soap batter in a variety of colors and then pouring these portions into a single pot in a pattern that can be either random or planned. The batter should not be mixed too much; if it is, the colors will blend into each other rather than generating distinct swirls. The key is to avoid mixing the batter too much. Once all of the different colors have been added to the pot, the soap maker will use a spatula or a spoon to give the batter a quick stir, which will result in subtle swirling motions. Following this step, the soap is poured into the mold, where the colors continue to swirl and interact with one another. The pattern that is produced as a result of cutting the soap into bars is organic and variable, with each bar displaying a design that is distinct from the others.

Other common techniques include the drop swirl, which involves pouring colored soap batter into a base layer from different heights. This method is also known as the drop swirl. The colored soap batter is poured into the mold, and as it does so, it penetrates the foundation layer and generates beautiful patterns that are fluid and resemble raindrops or waves. Soap maker are able to produce designs that are either more defined or more abstract by altering the height and angle of the pour. This approach allows for greater control over the positioning of the swirls, and it also allows for flexibility in the design process. The drop swirl technique is most effective when applied to a soap batter that is somewhat thick and retains its shape while still being fluid enough to allow the colors to merge together without any clumps. Using this method, soaps that have designs that are not only visually attractive but also distinctive are frequently created. These patterns are dramatic and eye-catching.

After the soap batter has been put into the mold, the hanger swirl technique takes the swirl technique to the next level by including the use of a tool, such as a wire or a bent hanger, to manipulate the soap mixture. Those soap maker who want to incorporate more intricate and layered designs into their soap will find this process to be a great choice. Following the pouring of the base layer and the colored soap into the mold, the soap maker will then put the hanger or wire into the soap and move it in a certain pattern, such as a figure-eight, a loop, or an S-curve. After the soap has been cut into bars, the hanger swirl process produces elaborate swirls that extend over multiple dimensions. These swirls can have the appearance of ribbons, feathers, or other abstract patterns. It is essential to keep the consistency of the soap batter at the appropriate level in order to achieve a successful hanger swirl. The batter must be thick enough to hold the design that is made by the hanger, but it must not be so thick that the tool cannot move through it without interruption.

One of the more complex swirl techniques is the Taiwan swirl, which is often referred to as the peacock swirl. This technique calls for a higher level of precision and patience than other swirl techniques. Pouring thin layers of soap of varying colors into the mold in either straight or diagonal lines is the method that is utilized in this approach. After pouring the soap, the soap maker will use a skewer or a thin tool to form symmetrical and flowing patterns by dragging the tool between the layers of soap. This process is repeated until the desired design is achieved. The finished product is a bar of soap that has a design that is quite elaborate and detailed, and it looks like the feathers of a peacock. Although the Taiwan swirl is a labor-intensive procedure that calls for a steady hand and takes a considerable amount of time, the finished product is a soap that is both visually appealing and extremely artistic.

Soap maker are able to create soaps with crisp, distinct bands of color or texture by employing another advanced design method known as layering. The process of layering involves pouring soap batter in stages to form distinct layers that do not mix together, in contrast to swirling, which involves the colors blending and interacting with one another. It is essential to maintain control of the consistency of the soap batter in order to ensure that each layer is poured at the appropriate moment in order to achieve good layering. It is possible that the layers will merge together if the batter is too thin, but if it is too thick, it may not pour evenly, which may result in layers that are uneven or lumpy. It is common practice for soap maker to wait for each layer to gradually harden before pouring the next one. This is done to guarantee that the lines between the layers are clear and distinct.

It is possible to include layers in soap designs in a variety of different ways, ranging from straightforward patterns that involve alternating colors to more intricate patterns that combine layers with swirls, embeds, or textures. While some soap maker achieve ombré effects by gradually lightening or darkening the color of each subsequent layer, others experiment with bold, contrasting colors to generate a striking visual impression. Both of these approaches are used to create ombré effects. In addition to utilizing a variety of colors, soap maker have the ability to add texture to their layers by including components such as exfoliants, botanicals, or glitter in between each layer. This provides the soap with an additional dimension, not just in terms of its aesthetic appeal but also in terms of the tactile feel that it provides when it is used.

In order to create even more intricate and one-of-a-kind soap designs, it is possible to combine the swirling and layering processes. As an illustration, a soap maker might begin by creating a foundation layer by means of a swirling technique and then proceed to pour a layer of solid color on top of that. Alternatively, they might alternate layers of solid color with layers of swirlable soap. The completion of this kind of design calls for meticulous planning and an in-depth comprehension of the ways in which various soap batters will react when they are layered on top of one another. It is possible for soap maker to create bars of soap that are not only visually appealing but also offer a diversity of textures and effects inside a single bar by combining multiple techniques.

It is important to note that the use of colorants is an integral part of both the swirling and layering processes. A broad variety of colorants are available to soap maker, including natural choices such as clays, micas, and botanicals, as well as synthetic pigments and dyes. Colorants can be used in the production of soap. The choice of colorants is determined by the effect that is intended, as certain colorants are better suited to particular processes or offer colors that are more stable and bright. Micas, for instance, are frequently utilized in swirling procedures due to the fact that they generate vibrant, shimmering hues that are able to maintain their shape adequately in the soap. Clays and botanicals, on the other hand, offer tones that are more subdued and natural but have the potential to produce an appearance that is more earthy or rustic. To achieve the desired effects, it is vital to have a solid understanding of how various colorants interact in soap. This is true regardless of whether the objective is to produce patterns that are bold and vibrant or designs that are subtle and elegant.

Moreover, fragrance is an essential component in the creation of sophisticated soap patterns. In spite of the fact that the aesthetic appeal of soap is frequently the first thing that people notice, the smell is what truly makes the experience of using soap memorable. It is possible for soap maker to employ a wide range of essential oils and fragrance oils to complement their patterns, so producing soaps that not only have a stunning appearance but also have an enticing aroma. The choice of fragrance can accentuate the theme or mood of the soap, whether it is a relaxing lavender-scented bar with delicate pastel swirls or an invigorating peppermint soap with strong, red-and-white layers. Both of these examples are examples of choices that can be made. It is essential to be aware that certain fragrances have the ability to speed up the trace process, which results in the soap batter being more viscous at a faster rate. This can have an impact on the ability to make delicate swirls or layers. Soap manufacturers have a responsibility to be aware of the scents they employ and how those fragrances may influence the design process.

Not only may the choice of mold affect the color and scent of the soap, but it can also have an effect on the final appearance of the container. The molds that soap maker use can range from straightforward rectangular or square molds to more complex silicone molds with intricate patterns or forms. Soap maker have a wide range of options to choose from. In order to establish how the soap pattern is dispersed across each bar, the size and form of the mold will be taken into consideration. For instance, a rectangular loaf mold enables the creation of long, sweeping swirls that are revealed when the soap is cut into slices, whereas individual cavity molds may yield designs that are smaller and more confined. In addition, soap maker have the ability to experiment with various mold configurations. For instance, they can divide a loaf mold into portions in order to generate diverse designs within a single batch of soap.

Controlling the temperature is another essential component in the creation of complex soap designs, particularly when working with techniques such as swirling and layering. The fluidity of the soap batter and the degree to which the colors will interact with one another are both influenced by the temperature of the soap batter. It is possible that the batter will become excessively thin if it is heated to an excessive degree, which will cause the colors to blend together, resulting in a muddy appearance. In the opposite direction, if the batter is allowed to cool down too much, it may thicken up too rapidly, making it impossible to create swirls or layers that are clean. It is imperative that soap maker carefully monitor the temperature of both the oils and the lye solution in order to guarantee that the soap achieves the appropriate consistency for the design that they have in mind. There are some soap maker who prefer to work at a lower temperature since it allows them to have more time to work, while there are others who may use a higher temperature for designs that require the soap to set more rapidly.

As a conclusion, the art of generating complex designs in soapmaking, such as swirls and layers, takes a combination of technical competence, imagination, and an awareness of how various substances and procedures interact with one another. If soap maker are able to perfect these techniques, they will be able to create soaps that are not only practical but also works of art that are visually attractive. The creative possibilities are virtually limitless, whether one chooses to employ straightforward swirl techniques or to combine a number of different design elements. A plain bar of soap can be transformed into a luxurious and one-of-a-kind creation by soap maker to the extent that they continue to push the boundaries of soap design. This can be accomplished by paying great attention to detail, experimenting with different colors and textures, and having a passion for the craft.

CHAPTER IV

Soaps for Skin Care

Soaps for Sensitive Skin

When making soaps for those with sensitive skin, the most important thing to keep in mind is to create products that are not only soft and nutritious but also free of any substances that could be considered harsh or irritating. People who have sensitive skin frequently experience discomfort or adverse responses when they use standard commercial soaps that contain synthetic chemicals, perfumes, and preservatives. Handmade soaps, particularly those that are formulated for sensitive skin, provide an option that places an emphasis on the utilization of natural, calming ingredients that are customized to the individual requirements of the skin. Creating soaps for sensitive skin requires careful selection of ingredients, conscious formulation, and testing to guarantee that the soap is not only successful at cleansing but also helps protect and nourish the skin's natural barrier. This is required to ensure that the soap is effective in cleansing the skin.

There are a number of different ways in which sensitive skin might present itself, including redness, dryness, itching, or allergic reactions to particular substances. Skin sensitivity can be caused by a number of different factors, such as genetics, environmental stressors, or even underlying medical problems like eczema or rosacea. These variables can all contribute to the development of skin sensitivity. It is, therefore, not possible to make soaps for sensitive skin using a one-size-fits-all approach; rather, it is necessary to have a grasp of the many sensitivities that exist as well as the ways in which different components might affect the skin. When it comes to the formulation of soaps for sensitive skin, one of the most important aspects is to minimize the presence of potential irritants and replace them with alternatives that are calming, mild, and beneficial to the skin's health.

A significant factor in defining the overall gentleness and moisturizing capabilities of soaps designed for sensitive skin is the base oils that are utilized in the formulation of these soaps. Because of the large amount of oleic acid that it contains, olive oil is one of the most popular alternatives for formulations that are intended for sensitive skin. Oleic acid helps to hydrate and soothe the skin without causing pores to become clogged. Additionally, olive oil possesses anti-inflammatory characteristics, which makes it an excellent choice for people who suffer from illnesses such as psoriasis or eczema. Additionally, coconut oil is a fantastic option; nevertheless, it should be utilized in a moderate manner. When applied in excessive amounts, coconut oil can dry the skin despite the fact that it contains cleaning characteristics. When developing a soap for sensitive skin, it is vital to find a balance between cleansing and hydrating. One way to prevent the soap from being too harsh is to reduce the amount of coconut oil that is used in the formulation.

Shea butter, which is particularly well-known for its highly nourishing and moisturizing properties, is yet another oil that is beneficial for sensitive skin. Both vitamins A and E, which are abundant in shea butter, offer protection against free radicals and aid in the regeneration of skin that has been damaged. The presence of cinnamic acid, a natural anti-inflammatory substance that can calm inflammation and redness, is another benefit of this product. It is common practice to combine shea butter with other oils in order to produce a bar of soap that is sufficiently hydrating, well-balanced, and soft enough to be used on sensitive skin on a daily basis. In a similar vein, avocado oil is another popular ingredient because of the high concentration of vitamins and fatty acids that it contains. These components assist in the process of skin regeneration and healing. Due to the fact that it contains emollient characteristics, it is especially well-suited for dry or sensitive skin types.

In addition, castor oil is an excellent ingredient to include in soaps designed for sensitive skin because it contributes to the formation of a creamy lather and offers additional hydration. It is true that castor oil is a viscous oil; nonetheless, it is effective when used in modest quantities to assist balance the other oils that are present in the formulation. As a result of its humectant characteristics, it draws moisture to the skin, which assists in maintaining its hydration. It is possible to make a soap that is not only washing but also nutritious and protective for sensitive skin by combining castor oil with other oils such as olive oil and shea butter.

In addition to selecting the appropriate base oils, it is essential to steer clear of the frequent irritants that are present in a great deal of commercial soaps. In particular, synthetic perfumes have the potential to be a significant trigger for individuals who have sensitive skin. A significant number of synthetic perfumes contain phthalates and other compounds that have the potential to generate allergic reactions or aggravate skin disorders. When it comes to people who have sensitive skin, the most effective method is to either utilize essential oils or leave the soap unscented. Essential oils such as chamomile, lavender, and calendula are well-known for their calming and soothing characteristics, which makes them good alternatives for formulations that are intended for sensitive skin. On the other hand, it is absolutely necessary to make use of these oils in modest doses, as even natural essential oils have the potential to stimulate irritation in certain individuals.

When making soaps for people with sensitive skin, the type of lye that is used is another factor to take into consideration. Although sodium hydroxide, also known as lye, is required for the saponification process in cold-process soapmaking, the end product must be carefully balanced to ensure that there is no free lye left in the soap. This is accomplished through the use of appropriate formulation, in which the oils and lye are combined in precise quantities in order to accomplish complete saponification. Additionally, a procedure known as super fatting can be utilized, which involves the addition of additional oils to the soap combination. This is done in order to guarantee that the final bar contains unreacted oils that offer the skin additional moisture and a softer texture. Due to the fact that it helps to guarantee that the soap does not become excessively drying and that it maintains its mild and moisturizing properties, super fatting is particularly useful for skin that is sensitive.

When making soap for those with sensitive skin, it is also very important to take into consideration the pH of the soap. When compared to the natural pH of the skin, which is approximately 5.5, soap normally has a pH level that is between 9 and 10, making it more alkaline. In spite of the fact that the alkaline composition of soap is essential for efficient cleansing, it may occasionally be too harsh for skin that is sensitive. It is possible to alleviate this problem by incorporating components such as aloe vera or oat milk into the soap. These components have the ability to calm the skin and bring the soap's pH level closer to the natural level of the skin. In particular, aloe vera possesses qualities that are both anti-inflammatory and therapeutic, making it an excellent choice for skin that is sensitive. It is also possible for the soap to have a silky texture due to its gel-like composition, which makes it soothing and smooth on the skin during use.

Colloidal oatmeal is yet another wonderful component that may be found in soaps designed for sensitive skin.

Including oatmeal in soap can provide soothing relief for conditions such as eczema, dermatitis, and other inflammatory skin issues. Oatmeal has been used for generations as a natural therapy for dry and irritated skin, and its inclusion in soap can provide this relief. You can create a gentle exfoliating effect while also relaxing the skin by incorporating colloidal oats into the soap recipe. This can be accomplished by grinding the oatmeal into a fine powder. Because of its ability to help lock in moisture and minimize inflammation, it is especially helpful for people who have skin that is dry or can cause itching.

Additionally, honey is a natural ingredient that might be beneficial to skin that is sensitive. Honey is a humectant, which means that it makes it easier for the skin to attract and hold onto moisture. Additionally, it possesses antimicrobial characteristics, which might be advantageous for persons who have skin that is prone to acne or that is inflamed. Soap that contains honey has a more rich texture, and it also has the potential to feel more moisturizing and relaxing. Honey, when used in moderation, has the potential to contribute to the creation of a soap that helps wash the skin without removing the skin's natural oils.

Due to the fact that it is both soothing and nutritious, goat's milk is another component that is frequently included in soaps designed for those with sensitive skin. Lactic acid, which is found in goat's milk, is a naturally occurring alpha-hydroxy acid (AHA) that assists in the removal of dead skin cells and encourages the turnover of tissues. On the other hand, in contrast to more effective chemical exfoliants, the lactic acid found in goat's milk is gentle and can be tolerated by skin that is sensitive. Additionally, goat's milk is abundant in fatty acids, proteins, and vitamins, all of which contribute to the conditioning and nourishment of the skin. Because it has a creamy consistency, the soap has a soft and gentle feel to it, making it an excellent option for individuals who have skin that is dry or inflamed from irritation.

In soaps designed for sensitive skin, clay is still another natural element that can be included; nonetheless, it is important to exercise caution when employed. It is common practice to incorporate clays such as kaolin and bentonite into soap in order to give a mild exfoliation and absorb excess oil without causing the skin to become stripped. For instance, kaolin clay is one of the clays that is considered to be the most mild. It can be used in tiny amounts to impart a velvety feel to the soap. People who have sensitive or reactive skin can use it because it helps to cleanse the skin without producing irritation, making it suited for those individuals. On the other hand, it is vital to avoid using an excessive amount of clay because, if used in excess, it can cause the skin to become dry.

In the process of making soaps for people with sensitive skin, it is particularly important to pay attention to the curing process. In order for the soap to completely harden and for any extra water to evaporate, handmade cold process soaps need to be allowed to cure for a period of time ranging from four to six weeks. As this period of time passes, the soap becomes less harsh and less prone to cause irritation to the skin. In the event that the curing process is rushed or the soap is used before it has reached its full cure, the end result may be a product that is too harsh for the skin that is sensitive. When it comes to making gentle soaps, patience is absolutely necessary because the right curing process guarantees that the soap will be effective, gentle, and long-lasting.

In the process of making soaps for sensitive skin, testing is another key issue to consider. Before applying the soap to a larger region of the skin, it is vital to perform a patch test on a small section of the skin. This is because sensitive skin can show reactions to even natural substances. As a result of this patch test, any potential allergies or irritants that may be present in the soap can be identified. In addition, it is beneficial to solicit input from individuals who have sensitive skin in order to guarantee that the soap is suitable for a larger percentage of the population. For the purpose of continuously improving their recipes and avoiding any problems in the future, soap maker should always keep records of their formulas and any comments they get.

In conclusion, the process of making soaps for sensitive skin needs a conscious approach to the selection of ingredients, the formulation, and the testing of the soap. Soap maker are able to create products that are soothing and protective for sensitive skin by concentrating on ingredients that are mild and nutritious, such as olive oil, shea butter, and essential oils. This allows them to avoid potential irritants, such as synthetic scents and harsh detergents. By super fatting the soap and carefully managing the pH, it is possible to further enhance the mildness of the soap, making it safe for everyday use on even the most sensitive skin. Crafting beautiful, effective soaps that cater to the specific requirements of individuals with sensitive skin can be accomplished by soap maker through a combination of artistic skill and scientific knowledge. These soaps provide those with sensitive skin with a safe and gentle alternative to commercial solutions.

Moisturizing Formulas

In the process of manufacturing handmade soaps, one of the most important aspects is the creation of moisturizing formulae. This is especially true for those individuals who want to supply their customers with goods that are both nourishing and hydrating. Moisturizing soaps are especially beneficial for people who have dry skin since they assist in restoring moisture to the skin, improve the texture of the skin, and improve the overall appearance of the skin. The composition of moisturizing soaps needs a careful selection of oils, butter, and additions that work together in harmony to produce the needed moisturizing effects while keeping the soap's cleansing capabilities. This is necessary in order to achieve the intended results. For the purpose of making moisturizing soaps that are successful, it is essential to have a solid understanding of the components that contribute to moisture retention, as well as the science behind these components.

Choosing the appropriate oils and fats is the first step in the process of making any kind of moisturizing soap. The moisturizing properties of the soap are primarily developed by oils, which are the major elements responsible for their creation. The fatty acids, vitamins, and antioxidants that are included in each oil are distinct from one another, and these differences can have an effect on the texture and efficacy of the finished product. By way of illustration, olive oil is well-known for its ability to moisturize the skin because of the high concentration of oleic acid that it contains. Oleic acid is able to deeply infiltrate the skin and offer hydration that is long-lasting. In addition to this, it has a high concentration of antioxidants, which are known to shield the skin from the damaging effects of oxidative stress and the aging process. In a similar vein, sweet almond oil is frequently used due to its lightweight consistency and high quantities of fatty acids, which enable it to be easily absorbed by the skin without leaving behind a greasy residue.

Coconut oil is still another good option for moisturizing soaps; however, its usage must be balanced with the use of other oils in order to prevent excessive dryness. When used in high doses, coconut oil can be drying despite the fact that it has excellent cleaning and lather characteristics. For this reason, soap maker frequently combine coconut oil with oils that are more hydrating, such as olive oil or avocado oil, in order to produce a balance that cleanses the skin without removing the skin's natural oils. Avocado oil, in particular, is an excellent option for moisturizing soaps since it contains a high concentration of fatty acids, vitamins, and antioxidants within its composition. Because of its high quantities of vitamins A, D, and E, it helps to maintain moisture levels and promotes cell regeneration, which are both beneficial to the health of the skin.

Additionally, the use of butter in the soap formulation can considerably boost the moisturizing properties of the soap, in addition to the selection of the appropriate oils. Because of their very emollient characteristics and rich, creamy textures, butter such as cocoa butter and shea butter are among the most popular available options. Since it is derived from the nuts of the shea tree, shea butter is well-known for the profound moisturizing capabilities that it possesses. This product is loaded with a wide range of healthy fatty acids, such as stearic and oleic acids, which are known to provide the skin with nourishment and protection. Furthermore, shea butter is abundant in vitamins A and E, which are beneficial to the health of the skin and offer protection against free radicals. The incorporation of shea butter into soap results in the production of a luscious and creamy lather that leaves the skin feeling supple and nourished.

Soaps that contain cocoa butter are another wonderful option for hydrating the skin. With its high melting point and rich, solid texture, this fat is produced from cacao beans. Because of its high melting point, it is an excellent choice for imparting creaminess and structure to soap bars. Stearic acid, which is abundant in cocoa butter, contributes to the formation of a protective barrier on the skin, which maintains the skin's hydration and prevents it from becoming dry. Additional benefits are provided by the natural antioxidants that are present in cocoa butter. These antioxidants protect the skin from the damaging effects of environmental influences. When cocoa butter is used in soap recipes, it not only imparts a wonderful chocolate scent but also improves the entire moisturizing experience.

Even while oils and butter are the foundation of moisturizing soap formulas, the inclusion of other components can further increase the hydration and nourishment that the soap offers to the skin. Honey and glycerin are two examples of humectants that are considered to be ideal additions to moisturizing soaps. The process of saponification results in the production of glycerin, which is a naturally occurring byproduct. Glycerin functions as a humectant because it draws moisture from the air closer to the skin. Because of this feature, glycerin is an extremely useful component in soap since it helps to keep the skin hydrated and prevents it from becoming dry and flaky. It is possible that the incorporation of glycerin into the composition will result in a soap that is more emollient, softer, and beneficial to the skin throughout the day.

Honey is yet another natural humectant that has the ability to enhance the moisturizing characteristics of soap. Honey, which is well-known for its antibacterial and antioxidant properties, has the ability to draw moisture into the skin while also delivering a calming and soothing effect. Because of its thick consistency, the soap gains a luxury texture, which ultimately results in a product that has a nourishing and sumptuous feel to it. When formulating honey, it is essential to take into consideration the possibility of caramelization, which might have an impact on the color and aroma of the soap. It is recommended that honey be added at trace or mixed into the soap base during the cooling portion of the process in order to prevent this from happening.

Soap compositions that are designed to moisturize the skin frequently contain aloe vera, which is another helpful element. The gel that is derived from the aloe vera plant is well-known for its ability to calm and hydrate the skin during and after use. It is rich in vitamins, minerals, and amino acids, all of which are beneficial to the health and repair of the skin. Aloe vera is especially beneficial for people who have skin that is sensitive or inflamed since it can provide relief and moisture without creating any extra irritation to the skin. When aloe vera is included in soap, it can be used either as a liquid ingredient or as an additive to produce a distinctive texture and a moisturizing effect.

In addition to oils, butter, humectants, and botanical additions, the moisturizing characteristics of soap can also be improved by the inclusion of a variety of plant extracts. As an example, chamomile extract is well-known for its relaxing and anti-inflammatory characteristics, which makes it an excellent choice for formulas specifically designed for sensitive skin. In a similar vein, calendula extract is frequently utilized in moisturizing soaps due to the calming and curative properties that it possesses. Not only do these extracts contribute to the overall effectiveness of the soap, but they also add natural colors and scents that can enrich the experience of using the soap.

The selection of the appropriate formulation is of the utmost importance in order to guarantee that the finished product will have the desired moisturizing benefits. In the process of creating moisturizing soaps, it is of utmost importance to strike a balance between the percentages of moisturizing oils, butter, and other components in order to produce a soap that is soothing to the skin while still being effective. If you want to produce a sufficient quantity of moisture without compromising the soap's ability to clean, the total oil weight should normally be constituted of anywhere between 20 and 40 percent of the whole formulation. It is common practice for soap maker to make use of a lye calculator in order to ascertain the perfect proportions of oils and lye. This is done in order to guarantee that the soap is well-balanced and free of any excess lye that can irritate the skin.

When it comes to the creation of moisturizing soaps, the curing process is yet another essential and significant consideration. It is necessary for the soap to go through a curing process that lasts for at least four to six weeks after it has been placed into molds. In this period of time, the excess moisture in the soap evaporates, which enables the soap to become more solid and produce its final texture. In addition, the process of curing enables the soap to become less harsh and more soothing on the skin, which guarantees that it will deliver the moisturizing advantages that were intended. If you rush the curing process, you can end up with a product that is excessively soft, prone to breaking or does not have the desired moisturizing effects.

The formulation of moisturizing soaps also includes testing, which is an important phase in the process. Tests should be performed on each batch of soap to determine how well it moisturizes different types of skin. This will ensure that the soap is able to fulfill the requirements of the people who will be using it. In order to uncover any potential problems or areas that could want improvement, soap maker can solicit feedback from other people, such as family and friends, or even through local marketplaces. As a result of this feedback, it is possible that modifications to the recipe will be required in order to produce a product that is positively received by all consumers.

The presentation of moisturizing soaps should also take into consideration the packaging, which is another important feature. It is important that the packaging conveys the premium character of the product while also offering sufficient protection against moisture and other external elements. Enhancing the overall appeal of the soap and attracting clients who are looking for moisturizing items can be accomplished through the use of options such as biodegradable wrappers, environmentally friendly boxes, or even transparent packaging. The visual presentation of the soap, in addition to any elements of branding, has the potential to play a key role in enticing potential purchasers and conveying the opulent attributes of the product.

In conclusion, giving careful thought to the formulation techniques and components that are utilized in the process of generating moisturizing formulae for handcrafted soaps is essential. Soap maker are able to create soaps that offer remarkable moisture and nourishment for the skin by including nourishing oils, luscious butter, and powerful humectants in their formulations. Soap maker are able to develop luxurious soaps that not only wash the skin but also enhance skin health and overall well-being because they successfully combine artistic expression with scientific research. Soap manufacturers may ensure that their moisturizing soaps suit the requirements of customers and stand out in a market that is very competitive by carefully formulating their products, allowing them to cure properly, and conducting tests. An experience that provides customers with a pampering experience that transforms their daily washing ritual into a moment of indulgence and self-care is the outcome of the creation of a product that represents the essence of luxury: handmade soap-making.

Exfoliating and Detox Soaps

In recent years, people have been increasingly conscious of the significance of skin health and the advantages of including specialized cleansing products in their skincare regimens. As a result, exfoliating and detox soaps have garnered a substantial amount of popularity. These kinds of soaps serve a dual purpose: not only do they clean the skin, but they also help remove dead skin cells and other impurities, which results in a complexion that is healthier and more radiant. It is necessary to have a grasp of the many substances that are capable of efficiently exfoliating the skin and drawing out toxins in order to formulate exfoliating and detox soaps. Additionally, it is necessary to have an understanding of the ways that can be used to incorporate these ingredients into the process of creating soap.

Exfoliation is a procedure that involves removing dead skin cells from the surface of the skin. This is in its most fundamental form. By exfoliating the skin on a regular basis, you may help prevent pores from becoming blocked, reduce the amount of acne that appears, and enhance the overall texture and appearance of the skin. Both physical and chemical exfoliation are the two basic types of exfoliation options. Chemical exfoliation makes use of acids or enzymes to break down the bonds that hold dead skin cells together, making it easier to remove them from the skin. Physical exfoliation, on the other hand, involves the use of abrasive materials to manually remove dead skin cells. When it comes to the creation of exfoliating soaps, it is possible to use a combination of the two approaches in order to get the best possible results, taking into account the various skin types and preferences.

Ground coffee, sugar, salt, oats, and a variety of seeds and nuts are some of the substances that can be found in physical exfoliants. These exfoliants are often sourced from natural sources. As a result of its gritty texture and energizing aroma, coffee grinds are particularly popular for use in the production of exfoliating soaps. They offer a particularly effective scrubbing action, which assists in the removal of dead skin cells while simultaneously boosting circulation and rejuvenating the skin. In addition, coffee possesses antioxidant characteristics that can be beneficial to the skin, which makes it an exceptionally desired component for use in body soaps as well as facial soaps. When developing soaps with coffee grounds, it is essential to take into consideration the coarseness of the grounds. This is because finer paper may be better suited for sensitive skin, whilst coarser paper offer a more thorough exfoliation for parts of the skin that are more resistant to exfoliation.

The use of sugar as an exfoliator is another efficient method that may be incorporated into soap ingredients. It is common knowledge that sugar scrubs are popular because of their gentle yet powerful exfoliating characteristics, which makes them suited for skin that is sensitive. When opposed to salt or coffee, sugar grains offer a more gentle exfoliation because they dissolve in water. As a result of this quality, sugar is an ideal choice for facial soaps, which are designed to be used on skin that is thinner and more delicate. In addition, sugar possesses humectant characteristics, which enable it to attract moisture to the skin. This, in turn, boosts the overall moisturizing effects that the soap has. When introducing sugar into soap formulations, it is vital to evaluate the optimum amount to utilize. This is because an excessive amount of sugar can result in a gritty texture and may cause the soap to become too soft.

An additional frequent exfoliant that can be utilized in the production of soap is salt. By providing a more intense exfoliation, it is frequently included in body scrubs and soaps that are targeted for parts of the body with coarser skin, such as the elbows and the feet. Salts such as sea salt, Himalayan salt, and Epsom salt are all popular choices, and each of these salts has a different mineral composition and set of advantages. The minerals that are abundant in sea salt have the ability to nourish the skin and assist in the removal of pollutants. Additionally, it possesses natural antimicrobial characteristics, which makes it advantageous for skin that is prone to acne. In order to prevent the skin from becoming overly dry, it is essential to strike a balance between the abrasive properties of salt and the moisturizing properties of other components when making soaps with salt.

The use of oats is yet another natural substance that has the potential to give exfoliating advantages. For instance, colloidal oatmeal is a kind of oats that has been finely powdered and is easily absorbed into soap formulas. Because of the calming effects that oatmeal is known to have, it is an excellent choice for skin that is sensitive or inflamed. All of these things lead to healthy skin, including the fact that it helps to absorb excess oil, gently exfoliate dead skin cells, and give hydration. Additionally, oatmeal has the ability to improve the texture of the soap, resulting in a creamy lather that has a rich feel when applied to the skin. In the process of formulating with oatmeal, it is essential to select the appropriate grind size in order to produce the desired level of exfoliation without being excessively unpleasant.

Chemical exfoliants, on the other hand, are characterized by the utilization of enzymes, alpha-hydroxy acids (AHAs), and beta-hydroxy acids (BHAs) in order to facilitate the process of exfoliation. Fruits and milk are the sources of water-soluble acids known as alpha-hydroxy acids (AHAs), which include glycolic and lactic acid. According to their mechanism of action, they break the connections that hold dead skin cells together, making it easier for those cells to shed. Because BHAs, like as salicylic acid, are oil-soluble and have the ability to infiltrate pores, they are ideal for treating acne-prone skin because of their effectiveness. By breaking down dead skin cells, enzymes, such as those derived from papaya and pineapple, give a gentle exfoliation that is beneficial to the skin. In the process of making exfoliating soaps, it is of the utmost importance to give careful consideration to the concentration of chemical exfoliants that are utilized. This is done to prevent irritation and to guarantee that the soap is acceptable for a wide range of skin types.

When it comes to the composition of exfoliating and detox soaps, the inclusion of detoxifying components is an essential component, in addition to the presence of exfoliating agents. When it comes to skincare, detoxification is the act of drawing out impurities, pollutants, and excess oils from the skin. Detoxification is a term that refers to the process of eliminating toxins from the body. With their natural adsorbent characteristics, many of the substances that are used in detoxification are able to bind to pollutants and assist in the cleansing of the skin. Activated charcoal is one of the most well-known substances that is used in soap production because of its detoxifying properties. As a result of its porous nature, which enables it to seek out and ensnare contaminants, it is an extremely efficient method for performing thorough cleansing. The use of activated charcoal can assist in the reduction of excess oil, the unclogging of pores, and an overall improvement in the clarity of the skin. On the other hand, it is vital to use activated charcoal in moderation because excessive use can lead to dryness or irritation, especially for skin types that are sensitive.

Bentonite clay, which is a natural clay that is generated from volcanic ash, is another famous component that is used for detoxification. Bentonite clay possesses exceptional absorbent capabilities, which enable it to extract toxins and impurities from the skin where they are present. Because it helps to reduce excess sebum and unclog pores, it is especially good for oily skin and skin that does not respond well to acne treatments. Bentonite clay, when incorporated into soap, has the potential to not only add to a creamy texture but also to boost the cleansing characteristics of the soap. For the purpose of preserving equilibrium and preventing the soap from becoming excessively dry, it is essential to blend clay with hydrating components.

Another detoxifying clay that is frequently used in soaps is called French green clay. As a result of its high mineral content and natural cleansing capabilities, it has the potential to effectively cleanse and revitalize the skin. It is possible for French green clay to assist in regulating oil production while also giving nutrients, making it suited for a wide range of skin types, including oily and combination skin. Additionally, the incorporation of clay into the soap not only improves its ability to cleanse the body but also contributes to the soap's aesthetic appeal by producing distinctive color variations and textures.

Herbal components, in addition to clay and activated charcoal, have the potential to boost the detoxifying effects of other compounds found in exfoliating soaps.

Examples of herbs that can be infused into soap include dandelion root and burdock root, both of which are known for their ability to cleanse the skin and can be used to produce cleaner skin. According to popular belief, these herbs have the ability to cleanse the blood and enhance circulation, both of which can have a beneficial impact on the appearance of the skin. When oils are infused with these plants, it is possible to create a healthy base for the soap, which also provides extra detoxification advantages.

In order to achieve the right balance of cleansing, exfoliation, and hydration, it is necessary to give great consideration to the overall formulation while making exfoliating and detoxifying soaps. A careful calculation should be made to determine the appropriate combination of physical and chemical exfoliants, as well as detoxifying substances, in order to accommodate different types of skin. In most cases, the total oil weight should make up between 20 and 40 percent of the composition. This will enable the skin to be well-cleansed without removing its natural moisture barrier. Due to the fact that a pH that is either too high or too low might cause irritation or dryness, it is also vital to make sure that the soap has a pH that is balanced.

It is possible to further improve the efficacy of exfoliating and detoxifying soaps by incorporating essential oils into the formulation. This not only imparts a nice aroma but also offers extra advantages related to the skin. As an illustration, tea tree oil is well-known for its antibacterial and antifungal qualities, which makes it a good choice for formulations that are intended for acne-prone skin formulations. Eucalyptus oil can help energize the senses and promote a sense of clarity, while lavender oil has calming effects that can soothe sore skin. Both of these oils can be discovered in essential oils. It is necessary to take into consideration the concentrations of essential oils when utilizing them in soap formulations. This is done to ensure that the essential oils continue to be safe and useful for the skin.

When it comes to the process of making exfoliating and detox soaps, one of the most important steps is testing the final recipe. The washing, exfoliating, and moisturizing capabilities of each batch have to be tested on distinct skin types in order to ensure that they are effective. It is possible to gain useful insights and assist in identifying any potential problems that may need to be addressed by collecting feedback from users. In order to develop a product that caters to the requirements of a wide range of consumers, it is possible that the formulation will require some modifications based on the findings of the tests.

The process of curing is also necessary for the production of exfoliating and detoxifying soaps. Immediately following the pouring of the soap into molds, it is recommended that the soap be allowed to cure for a period of four to six weeks. This will allow any excess moisture to evaporate and the soap to harden properly. In addition, this time period enables the chemical interactions to become more stable, which ultimately results in a solution that is less harsh and more gentle, and which effectively cleanses and exfoliates without stimulating irritation. When the curing process is rushed, the result may be a soap that is excessively gentle or harsh, which may compromise the overall quality and efficiency of the finished product.

To conclude, the packaging of exfoliating and detox soaps should not only provide enough protection against moisture and external conditions, but it should also reflect the exquisite quality of the product itself. Think about using environmentally friendly packaging solutions that draw attention to the natural components that are employed in the recipe. Customers are drawn to products that are visually appealing, and clear packaging might be used to showcase the distinctive colors and textures of the soap, which would attract said customers. Additionally, consumers can be educated and their experience with the product can be improved by using labeling that is educational and that highlights the benefits of the substances.

In conclusion, the process of making exfoliating and detox soaps calls for a careful approach to the selection of ingredients and the formulation procedures. Soap makers are able to develop solutions that efficiently wash, exfoliate, and revitalize the skin by mixing physical and chemical exfoliants with substances that detoxify the skin. There is a mix of moisturizing and detoxifying characteristics in the finished product, which ensures that it is suitable for a wide range of skin types and provides a cleansing experience that is both luxurious and useful. It is possible for soap makers to develop wonderful exfoliating and detox soaps by carefully formulating, testing, and paying attention to detail. These soaps provide customers with an indulgent and effective addition to their skincare routine.

CHAPTER V

Personalizing Your Soap

Blending Scents

A delicate craft that requires imagination, knowledge of fragrance qualities, and an awareness of how different scents interact with each other and with the skin, blending scents in soap production is a complex process that requires a lot of attention to detail. Not only can the creation of beautiful soaps with harmonious aromas improve the sensory experience of using the product, but it also has the potential to elicit feelings and memories and even alter mood to a certain extent. Scent blending is a procedure that involves selecting essential oils, fragrance oils, and other aromatic compounds and then carefully combining them in proportions that enable the creation of a smell profile that is well-rounded and appealing. The principles of fragrance composition, the selection of acceptable ingredients, the methods of blending, and the impact of scent on the user experience are all topics that are discussed in this section, which goes into the complexities of blending scents for the purpose of manufacturing soap.

It is vital for any soap producer who wants to generate complex and enticing smell profiles to have a fundamental understanding of the composition of fragrances. It is common practice to classify fragrances into three notes: the top note, the middle note, and the base note. Top notes are the first smells that are detected when a soap is used for the first time. Top notes are often light, fresh, and volatile, and they evaporate very rapidly. Herbal fragrances such as basil and peppermint are examples of top notes. Citrus oils such as lemon and lime are also examples of top notes. When the top notes begin to fade, the middle notes, which are often referred to as heart notes, begin to form and add to the body of the fragrance. In general, these fragrances have a more rounded quality and may contain floral components like jasmine or lavender, as well as spice undertones like cinnamon. The base notes give the aroma a sense of depth and longevity, and they remain on the skin even after the soap has been used. Scents such as sandalwood, patchouli, and vanilla are examples of fragrances that are typically described as being deep, heavy, and anchoring. The successful blending of fragrances involves a careful balance of all three types of notes. This allows the soap to deliver a unified scent experience from the very first whiff to the very last perfume that lingers on the skin.

When it comes to combining scents, it is essential to choose the appropriate materials. The use of essential oils, which are obtained from plants through a variety of processes such as steam distillation or cold pressing, is the most natural option for soap manufacturers who are interested in producing luxurious products. Each essential oil has its own distinctive aroma profile and medicinal characteristics that are exclusive to it. For instance, lavender essential oil is well-known for its relaxing effects, and tea tree oil is highly recognized for its antibacterial properties. Both of these oils are essential oils. On the other hand, fragrance oils are synthetic or mixed fragrances that are designed to resemble natural aromas. They can come in a broad variety of possibilities, some of which can be more stable and longer-lasting than essential oils in soap compositions. Fragrance oils are widely used in the cosmetics industry. Furthermore, fragrance oils can provide complex mixtures that may be difficult to accomplish with essential oils alone, allowing for a greater variety of creative expression. This is why fragrance oils are becoming increasingly popular. In order to get the aroma profiles that they like, many soap makers opt to employ a combination of essential oils and fragrance oils. This allows them to strike a balance between the genuineness of natural fragrances and the adaptability of synthetic scents.

Experimenting with different smell combinations is the next stage for the soap maker after they have finally decided on the components they will use. For the purpose of determining the optimal balance and quantity of various oils, this process frequently entails the creation of test batches. It is usual practice to begin the blending process by utilizing a base note as the foundation, followed by the addition of middle notes, and ultimately the incorporation of top notes to complete the blend. It is recommended to work in modest increments, adding a few drops at a time, and allowing the mixture to rest for a short length of time in order to properly develop before making any additional modifications. This interval of repose allows the fragrances to combine, which is necessary because different oils have varied reactions when they are combined. In addition, soap makers frequently maintain a comprehensive record of their mixtures, documenting the amounts of each oil that was used, the final aroma profile, and any notes regarding the development of the fragrance over the course of time. In the process of duplicating successful blends or improving ones that were less successful, this documentation can prove to be of great value.

When blending fragrances for soap, it is also essential to have a solid understanding of how the aroma affects the overall experience of the consumer. Due to the fact that scent has the ability to elicit powerful emotional responses and memories, it is a vital component of the overall experience of using the product. As an illustration, flowery fragrances have the potential to elicit sentiments of romanticism or peace, whilst citrus fragrances have the ability to enliven and energize. It is also possible that particular aromas possess therapeutic characteristics, which can have an effect on the user's state of mind and overall well-being. Aromatherapy has been demonstrated to have the ability to alter both psychological and physiological reactions, such as lowering levels of stress and anxiety levels, according to research. When soap makers take the time to properly pick and combine smells, they are able to produce products that not only smell lovely but also improve the overall experience of using the soap. When manufacturers have a better knowledge of the relationship between scent and emotion, they are better able to create mixes that resonate with their target audience, whether they are trying to achieve a sensation of relaxation, invigoration, or nostalgia.

The manner in which aromas are combined is yet another essential aspect to take into consideration. Before incorporating fragrances into the soap base, it is usual practice to first combine them in a carrier oil using a soapmaking technique. Using this method not only helps to ensure that the fragrances are distributed uniformly throughout the soap but also gives the soap maker the opportunity to evaluate the fragrance before committing it to a larger batch. There is a possibility that the final perfume profile will be affected by the type of carrier oil that is utilized since certain oils have the ability to impart their aroma or alter the overall fragrance experience. As an illustration, the utilization of a carrier oil that possesses a potent aroma, like coconut oil, has the potential to modify the perceived intensity of the aromas that are applied. On the other hand, neutral oils such as sweet almond oil enable the blended scents to shine without any interference while they are being combined.

During the process of manufacturing soap, the timing of when scents are added can also have an effect on the aroma that is produced in the end. When making cold-process soap, essential oils, and fragrance oils are normally added after the oils and lye have been mixed together and emulsified. Because the heat that is generated during the saponification process might reduce the intensity of certain volatile notes, this scheduling helps to ensure that the smells are preserved in their original state. When manufacturing soap using the hot process, it is possible to add fragrances toward the end of the cooking process in order to prevent the fragrances from being absorbed by the temperatures. The addition of fragrances can be made in the process of creating melt and pour soap right before the base of the melted soap is poured into molds. When the appropriate timing is understood, it guarantees that the perfumes will continue to be vivid and faithful to the characteristics that were intended for them.

Furthermore, it is essential to take into consideration the aesthetic features that come into play while combining scents, in addition to the technical ones that are involved. The way in which the soap is presented visually has the potential to improve the user's experience across the board. The color of the soap, the design of the mold, and even the packaging can all be considered part of this category. A bar of soap that is exquisitely crafted can contribute to the creation of an alluring visual experience that is in harmony with its aroma. An example of this would be a soap with a citrus aroma that is brilliant yellow in color, which would evoke emotions of freshness and sunshine. On the other hand, a lavender soap that is intended to be calming could be presented in gentle purple tones. Through careful presentation and design, the sensory appeal of the soap can be enhanced, so reinforcing the exquisite experience that soap manufacturers strive to give for their customers.

When it comes to combining smells, another important factor to take into consideration is the safety and regulatory implications of using different fragrance compounds. There are a variety of skin sensitivities that can be caused by essential oils and fragrance oils; therefore, it is essential for soap producers to have a thorough understanding of the qualities of the materials they are employing. Certain oils have the potential to irritate the skin of certain persons, particularly when they are applied to delicate skin types or when they are used in higher quantities. It is of the utmost importance to carry out an exhaustive study on the maximum safe usage rates for each oil and to adhere to the rules established by the industry for cosmetic formulations. As an additional measure, manufacturers of soap ought to take into account the possibility of allergic responses and provide transparent labeling that lists all of the fragrance components that are utilized in their goods. In order to cultivate trust with customers and guarantee a pleasant experience, it is beneficial to be open and honest about the components that make up soap.

Modern soap manufacturers are increasingly taking into consideration the concept of sustainability when it comes to the process of combining smells. As people become more conscious of environmental problems, a growing number of consumers are searching for environmentally friendly items that are in line with their beliefs. This can have an effect on the selection of ingredients since an increasing number of soap manufacturers are using essential oils and fragrance oils that are sourced in a sustainable manner and are in accordance with ethical principles. Soap manufacturers can appeal to a more ethical consumer base while simultaneously making a beneficial contribution to the world by using components that are manufactured in a way that minimizes the impact that they have on the environment.

There is no possible way to overestimate the relevance of smell blending when it comes to soap production. In order to successfully complete this procedure, you need to have a deep awareness of the composition of fragrances, the characteristics of different oils, and the emotional influence that scent has. The skill of combining smells enables soap makers to produce exquisite products that offer a multi-sensory experience, engaging not only the sense of smell but also the senses of sight and touch when used in conjunction with one another. In order to create distinctive and captivating aromas that set their goods apart from those of their competitors, soap makers can discover these fragrances by experimenting with a variety of different combinations and procedures.

To summarize, the process of combining smells for the purpose of making luxury soaps is a challenging and satisfying undertaking that requires a combination of artistic skill, scientific knowledge, and an in-depth comprehension of the sensory experience. Because of the careful selection of essential oils and fragrance oils, the rigorous blending procedures, and the awareness of the emotional and physical consequences of aroma, soap makers are able to create products that are both delightful and inspiring. Soap manufacturers are able to create one-of-a-kind and sumptuous goods that resonate with customers on several levels because of this sophisticated process, which, despite being tough, offers an infinite number of possibilities for creativity and invention. When it comes to making soaps that truly enrich the experience of handmade beauty for everyday use, the art of scent blending continues to be an essential component. This is true regardless of whether the objective is to elicit feelings of warmth and comfort, to invigorate the spirit, or to generate a sense of nostalgia.

Adding Botanicals

The use of botanicals in soap is a time-honored process that has been around for centuries and continues to be a highly valued component of contemporary soap-making. There is a vast variety of plant-based materials that are included in the category of botanicals. These materials include flowers, herbs, leaves, roots, seeds, and even fruits. They have the ability to dramatically improve the aesthetic, sensory, and functional properties of soap, which enables manufacturers to develop really opulent products that are not only aesthetically pleasing but also helpful to the skin and the psyche. The different features of adding botanicals to soap are discussed in this section. These aspects include the types of botanicals that are utilized, the advantages that they provide, the techniques of incorporation, the potential obstacles that may arise, and the artistic considerations that put botanical-infused soaps in a distinctive category.

Botanicals can be generically classified into a number of different categories, each of which possesses a certain set of characteristics and advantages. Flowers, which contribute both aroma and color to the finished product, are among the most widely utilized botanicals in the soap-making industry. Lavender, chamomile, and rose petals are examples of common floral botanicals. Each of these plants has a uniquely scented and visually appealing floral appearance. Lavender, for instance, is a wonderful option for relaxing the skin because it not only has a perfume that is comforting but also possesses characteristics that are anti-inflammatory and antibacterial. To a similar extent, rose petals can lend an air of sophistication and opulence to soap, while the natural oils that they contain have the ability to hydrate and nourish the skin. Additionally, natural herbs and botanicals, such as rosemary, mint, and basil, are utilized quite regularly. Not only can these herbs contribute distinctive aromas, but they may also have therapeutic properties, such as allowing circulation to be stimulated or having a cooling impact. Additionally, plants and seeds such as ginger, turmeric, and oats can be incorporated for their exfoliating capabilities, which can improve the texture of the soap while also offering benefits to the skin.

The incorporation of botanicals into soap affords a multitude of advantages. A big advantage is the increase of the soap's sensory profile, which is one of the most important advantages. In addition to offering delicious scents, visual attractiveness, and a pleasing texture, botanicals have the potential to enhance the overall experience of using the soap significantly. A regular bar of soap can be elevated to the level of a premium product that stimulates several senses through the use of botanicals during the manufacturing process. Additionally, a great number of botanicals include a high concentration of vitamins, minerals, and antioxidants that are beneficial to the skin. For example, aloe vera is well-known for its calming and hydrating effects, which is why it is frequently used in mild soaps that are made for skin that is sensitive. The anti-inflammatory and relaxing properties of chamomile make it an ideal ingredient for treatments that are designed to treat skin that is irritated or inflamed. Chamomile is frequently used in herbal remedies. Particular botanicals, such as eucalyptus and peppermint, can give aromatherapeutic effects, which can promote relaxation or invigoration while they are being used. This is in addition to the benefits that they provide for the skin.

It is necessary to give great consideration to the procedures that are utilized as well as the form of botanicals that are chosen when incorporating botanicals into soap. The addition of botanicals can be accomplished in a number of different ways, and the method that is selected can have an effect on the finished product's appearance, aroma, and texture. Infusing oils with botanicals before adding them to the soap composition is a process that is frequently used. This technique makes it possible to extract the beneficial elements of the botanicals into the carrier oil, which can subsequently be utilized in the process of creating soap. By way of illustration, the production of an olive oil infusion with dried chamomile flowers can result in an oil that is both calming and fragrant, so contributing to the overall quality of the finished soap. Both cold infusion and hot infusion are methods that can be utilized to create infusions. Cold infusion involves the botanicals being steeped in oil for a considerable amount of time, while hot infusion involves the application of mild heat in order to speed up the extraction process.

Directly incorporating dried botanicals into the soap formulation is still another option that can be taken. It is necessary to select botanicals that are stable and appropriate for use in soap in order to accomplish this, but they can add visual appeal and texture to the final product. It is possible to incorporate powdered botanicals, dried flowers, and herbs into the soap batter during the trace stage of the cold process soap production process. This is the stage at which the mixture has thickened to the point where it can retain the botanicals in suspension without allowing them to sink to the bottom. Experimentation and testing are essential in order to achieve the desired result since it is essential to keep in mind that the saponification process can cause certain botanicals to lose their color or scent. For instance, dried lavender buds are able to keep their color and aroma intact, whereas other botanicals, such as calendula petals, may have their color become more subdued following the saponification process. In order to account for these variances, soap manufacturers ought to be aware of them and modify their compositions accordingly.

The addition of botanicals as ornamental components is another possibility. For instance, a visually attractive finish can be achieved by placing fresh or dried flowers on top of the soap immediately before it is allowed to harden. This approach not only improves the cosmetic attractiveness of the soap but also gives the user the ability to recognize the aroma of the soap or the primary components that it contains. Nevertheless, when utilizing fresh botanicals, it is important to take caution in order to guarantee that the moisture content does not disrupt the process of the soap curing or cause it to go bad. In addition, manufacturers of soap should take into consideration the possibility that botanical ingredients will have an effect on the shelf life of the soap as well as the storage needs. Because of their consistency and durability, dried botanicals are frequently picked over fresh ones.

In spite of the fact that the incorporation of botanicals has the potential to improve the quality of soap, it also contains possible difficulties that soap makers ought to be aware of. In the course of the saponification process, there is a possibility that the botanical components will become discolored or deteriorate, which is a cause for concern. Certain botanicals have the ability to alter the color of the soap or eliminate its aroma, while others have the potential to cause the soap to go bad if it is not dried or maintained properly. Soap manufacturers frequently undertake small test batches in order to examine the behavior of the botanicals throughout the saponification process. This is done in order to reduce the negative effects of these hazards. Through the use of this kind of trial and error, they are able to fine-tune their formulas and determine which botanicals are most effective in their particular recipes.

Additionally, it is of the utmost importance to take into consideration whether or not the botanicals are compatible with the overall formulation of the soap. It is possible for some botanicals to react in a different manner when coupled with particular oils or additives, which might have an impact on the final qualities and texture of the soap. In the event that some powdered herbs are not adequately mixed into the soap, for instance, the lather of the soap may be affected, and the texture may become gritty. Consequently, in order to achieve a harmonic blend, it is essential to have a solid understanding of the qualities of the selected botanicals.

When viewed from an artistic point of view, the incorporation of botanicals into soap presents an infinite number of chances for creativity and customization. When it comes to appealing to customers who are looking for items that are visually spectacular, the aesthetic side of soap production plays a key part. Soap makers are able to create visually attractive bars that are reflective of their artistic vision if they carefully select botanicals after giving careful consideration to the colors, shapes, and textures of the botanicals. For instance, a soap that is embellished with colorful marigold flowers can create emotions of warmth and sunshine, whilst a lavender-infused soap that has delicate purple buds can indicate feelings of calm and tranquility. It is also possible to increase the visual appeal of botanicals by employing a variety of techniques, such as layering soaps of varying colors or whirling botanicals inside the soap batter to produce beautiful designs.

Botanicals, in addition to their visual and sensory qualities, can also contain symbolic connotations or cultural value, which adds an additional layer of complexity to the process of manufacturing soap. As an illustration, some flowers, such as hibiscus, are linked to feelings of love and passion, but sage is frequently associated with feelings of purification and cleanliness. The incorporation of these botanicals into soap has the potential to communicate a narrative or goal, so enabling manufacturers to develop goods that are in tune with particular concepts or principles. This connection to meaning has the potential to improve the experience of the user, elevating the function of the soap from that of a simple washing product to that of a production that is both meaningful and intentional.

If you want your botanical-infused soaps to be successful, marketing and branding are two of the most important factors. Customers are looking for items that are in line with their beliefs regarding the importance of wellness and sustainability, and they are increasingly drawn to natural and handmade products that place an emphasis on the utilization of botanicals. In order to attract a particular audience and communicate the distinctive attributes of the product, it is possible to highlight the botanical elements that are used in soap. For the purpose of engaging customers and establishing trust, soap manufacturers can tell their tales about the botanicals they source, the procedures they use to make soap, and the advantages of each component. By providing clients with information regarding the characteristics of the botanicals that are utilized, it is possible to assist them in making well-informed purchasing selections and to improve their entire experience with the product.

At the same time that the trend for personalization is expanding, the growing popularity of soaps that contain botanical ingredients is also developing. The fact that a large number of customers are looking for items that are tailored to their own requirements and tastes has prompted soap manufacturers to provide individualized possibilities. Consumers are able to create a sense of ownership and connection to the product by selecting their preferred smells, colors, and even specific skin advantages through the use of customizable botanical mixtures. It is possible for soap makers to cultivate a more profound relationship with their consumers by providing them with individualized soap-making experiences, such as seminars or online consultations. This gives customers the opportunity to learn more about the art of soap-making.

The use of botanicals provides eco-conscious soap producers with an option to find ingredients that are in line with their environmental ideals, which is an important aspect of sustainability. Due to the fact that many botanicals can be cultivated locally, the carbon footprint that is linked with the sourcing of materials can be reduced. In addition, the utilization of dried botanicals helps to reduce the amount of waste generated by packaging and promotes the utilization of natural, biodegradable components. Making soap that prioritizes sustainable practices not only has the potential to appeal to a growing market of consumers who are environmentally conscious, but it also has the potential to positively contribute to the communities in which they operate by supporting local agriculture and ethical sourcing.

In spite of the fact that the community of soap makers is always evolving, the incorporation of botanicals continues to be an essential component of the trade. Adding botanicals to soap has a wide range of potential applications, including increasing sensory experiences, boosting skin benefits, and encouraging creativity. These are just some of the interesting possibilities. Makers continue to experiment with a wide variety of botanical ingredients, processes, and design approaches, which contributes to the depth and diversity of the culture surrounding handmade soap.

As a conclusion, the incorporation of botanicals into soap is a complex and gratifying undertaking that enhances the visual and sensory attributes of the finished product. It is possible for soap makers to create luxury and meaningful soaps that engage with customers on numerous levels by carefully selecting the ingredients, incorporating them in a deliberate manner, and having a profound grasp of the qualities of the various botanicals employed. A connection to nature, the ability to express one's creativity, and the possibility of offering clients high-quality products that are beneficial to their well-being are all opportunities that can be provided by the art of manufacturing soap with botanical ingredients. It is still a key component in the production of beautiful soaps that offer joy, health, and inspiration to everyday life, despite the fact that the community of soap makers continues to embrace the beauty and advantages of botanicals.

Packaging and Presentation

When it comes to the soap-making sector, packaging and presentation are extremely important features since they serve not only as protective measures but also as marketing tools that transmit the essence of a product. It is possible for the manner in which soap is packaged to have a considerable impact on the perceptions of consumers, the identity of the brand, and, ultimately, sales for small businesses and artisans. Because the market for handmade soap is expected to continue expanding, it is becoming increasingly necessary to have a solid understanding of the fundamentals of successful packaging and presentation. The purpose of this section is to investigate many aspects of packaging and presentation in the soap-making process. These factors include materials, design considerations, branding, sustainability, and the emotional connection that may be created by products that are presented in an attractive manner.

In the process of creating soap, the selection of materials for the packaging is of the utmost importance. When storing and transporting soap, it is necessary to do it in a manner that safeguards it against exposure to light, moisture, and physical harm. Materials such as paper, cardboard, glass, plastic, and metal are frequently used for packing purposes. There are various benefits and drawbacks associated with each substance, and the selection of one will frequently be determined by the formulation of the soap, the target market, and the desired physical appearance. For instance, cardboard boxes or paper wraps can give the impression of being rustic and natural, which is a look that is ideally suited to organic or handmade items. When it comes to sustainability, these materials are frequently biodegradable and have the potential to improve perceptions. Glass jars or containers, on the other hand, might give the impression of being more opulent. These materials are typically utilized for specialty soaps like whipped body soaps, which require a more sophisticated presentation.

It is possible that plastic packaging is seen as being less environmentally friendly despite the fact that it is practical due to its lightweight and moisture-resistant characteristics. Nevertheless, developments in biodegradable polymers and recyclable materials are causing a shift in consumer expectations. These developments are enabling soap manufacturers to keep their products functional while simultaneously appealing to customers who are ecologically concerned. Soap manufacturers should take into consideration not just the functional features of the materials they choose for their packaging but also how well the materials connect with their brand identity and the market they are trying to reach.

When it comes to communicating the message of the business and being appealing to potential customers, the design of the packaging is of equal importance. In order to be effective, the design of the package should convey the essence of the product while also offering clear information about the advantages, ingredients, and use of the soap. There are a number of components that contribute significantly to the creation of appealing packaging, including color, font, and picture. For instance, a product that is characterized by soft pastel colors may be perceived as being soothing and peaceful, whereas bold hues may elicit sensations of energy and enthusiasm. Typography should be selected in such a way that it reflects the personality of the company; for example, elegant fonts may provide the impression of luxury, whilst playful and whimsical fonts might represent an attitude that is both fun and creative.

Including imagery on the product's packaging can further increase its appeal by offering visual cues that are likely to resonate with the audience that is being targeted. It is possible that this could include photographs of the soap itself, photographs of the botanical ingredients, or photographs of lifestyles that inspire sensations linked with using the product. For instance, in order to establish an emotional connection with customers, the package of a laundry detergent containing lavender can include pictures of lavender fields or other soothing scenery. In order to ensure that all of the components work together to produce a coherent brand image that is easily recognizable, the overall style should be harmonious.

When it comes to packaging and presentation, branding is an essential component since it develops the identity of the soap manufacturer and differentiates their products from those of their competitors. The ability of consumers to engage with a product on a deeper level, so improving their entire experience and strengthening their loyalty to the brand, can be facilitated by a powerful brand story. It is important for artisans to think about what makes their soaps unique, whether it be the ingredients that are used, the method that is used to make them, or the principles that underpin the brand. It is possible to communicate this narrative to customers through the design of the packaging, the labeling, and the marketing materials, which will enable them to comprehend the distinctive characteristics of the product that they are acquiring.

Additionally, soap manufacturers have the chance to educate customers about their products through the packaging used for their products. Labeling that is easy to understand and includes information about the components, the advantages of those components, and any distinctive characteristics can assist customers in making well-informed purchasing decisions. Additionally, transparency in labeling helps to cultivate trust, which is of utmost significance in this day and age, when customers are becoming more aware of and worried about the components that are contained in the personal care items they purchase.

The significance of the emotional connection that is established by packaging cannot be emphasized. Packaging that is thoughtfully designed has the ability to elicit sentiments of nostalgia, luxury, or well-being, so impacting the perceptions and experiences of consumers. This emotional response can be especially potent in the market for handmade soap, where products are frequently viewed as gifts or as objects for self-care. A simple bar of soap may be transformed into a treasured gift via the use of thoughtfully designed packaging, which also makes the process of unwrapping the product feel more special and memorable. It is possible to improve the tactile experience by incorporating components like texture, embossing, or distinctive closures into the packaging. This will make the package itself a part of the total enjoyment of the product.

Another important factor to take into account when packing and presenting products is sustainability. With customers becoming more aware of environmental issues, there has been an increase in the number of consumers looking for items that are in line with their values. Soap manufacturers have the opportunity to benefit from this trend by utilizing sustainable resources, reducing waste, and implementing policies that are good for the environment. Customers who are concerned about the environment may be interested in purchasing products that come in recyclable or biodegradable packaging. Additionally, techniques such as minimalistic packaging or refills can help reduce waste. Additionally, the narrative that is associated with sustainability efforts can be incorporated into the brand narrative, which enables customers to feel good about their purchases and to show their support for firms that place an emphasis on the environment.

In addition to the use of environmentally friendly materials, the manufacturing process of the packaging can also have an effect on the way it affects the environment. For the sake of lowering emissions from transportation and bolstering local economies, artisans should give serious consideration to purchasing their packaging from local vendors. It is possible to further improve a brand's reputation by collaborating with manufacturers who place a priority on ethical labor standards and ecologically friendly methods. Consumers who place high importance on ethical considerations in their purchasing decisions may respond positively to transparency regarding the techniques of production and the sources of the goods.

Furthermore, the presentation of soap involves not only the packaging of the product but also the manner in which it is shown and promoted. When soap manufacturers sell their wares at craft fairs, markets, or online, the manner in which they organize their products can have a considerable impact on the behavior of customers. Attracting attention and encouraging purchases can be accomplished through the use of a visually appealing display that highlights the colors, textures, and distinctive characteristics of the soap. Enhancing the presentation by utilizing decorations, signs, and lighting can help create an engaging ambiance that attracts customers to check out the business.

When it comes to online sales, it is crucial to have high-quality pictures and appealing product descriptions in order to effectively communicate the qualities of the soap to potential customers. Providing clients with clear photographs that emphasize the product's texture, colors, and packaging can assist them in visualizing the goods, which in turn increases the likelihood that they will complete a transaction. A well-considered presentation on e-commerce platforms has the potential to improve the shopping experience by facilitating a smooth transition from online browsing to the delivery of products.

In a world where customers are inundated with options, it is essential for a business to differentiate itself in the market in order to achieve success. Therefore, soap manufacturers have the chance to build a distinctive brand, establish a connection with their target audience, and separate themselves from other competitors through the use of packaging and presentation. Consumer views and purchasing behavior can be strongly influenced by a brand story that has been carefully established, a design that has been thoughtfully crafted, and attention to sustainability.

An additional emphasis has been placed on the significance of packaging and presentation as a result of the incorporation of social media into marketing initiatives. A brand's online presence can be improved by using visually appealing packaging, which can be done through platforms such as Instagram, Pinterest, and

Facebook, which have become significant tools for consumer product promotion. Sharing and engagement can be encouraged through the use of high-quality photographs of nicely packed soaps, which can ultimately lead to more visibility and new sales prospects. By engaging with customers through social media, soap manufacturers are able to collect feedback on the designs of their packaging and presentation techniques, which enables them to adapt their approach based on the preferences of their customers.

Additionally, expanding a brand's exposure and reputation can be accomplished through the involvement of influencers or artisans working in similar industries. Co-branded packaging or one-of-a-kind product offers that appeal to a wider audience might be the result of collaborations between two or more companies. It is common for influencers to have devoted followers, and the endorsement of a product by an influencer can have a major impact on the purchases that consumers make. It is possible to generate chances for cross-promotion and collaborative marketing efforts by cultivating relationships within the community of artisans.

Furthermore, the necessity of packaging and presentation will continue to be of the utmost importance as the soap-making sector continues to undergo transformations. Customers are looking for experiences that are congruent with their preferences and beliefs, and they are increasingly asking for more than just items that fulfill their functional needs. When combined with a compelling brand story and a focus on sustainability, carefully produced packaging has the potential to facilitate the formation of an emotional connection that, in turn, encourages customer loyalty and subsequent purchases. As soap manufacturers manage the challenges of packaging and presentation, they have the opportunity to develop goods that not only fulfill the utilitarian demands of their clients but also enrich their lives via intelligent design and meaningful relationships. This is a win-win situation for everyone involved.

In conclusion, the packaging and presentation of soap are essential elements of the manufacturing process that have an impact on the views and actions of consumers about their desire to purchase soap. Soap manufacturers are able to achieve their goal of producing products that stand out in a market that is highly competitive by carefully selecting materials, designing appealing packaging, and establishing a strong brand identity. It is possible to further boost the appeal of a brand by putting an emphasis on ethical standards and sustainability, which will attract consumers who are environmentally sensitive. It is possible for a simple product to be elevated to the status of a treasured item by the emotional connection that is formed through packaging. This can build loyalty and encourage repeat purchases. It will be crucial for artists who want to make their mark and connect with customers in a meaningful way to have a solid understanding of the fundamentals of good packaging and presentation as the handmade soap business continues to expand. Not only are soap makers able to craft beautiful soaps, but they can also craft experiences that are memorable and resonate with their audience by utilizing innovation, creativity, and a devotion to quality.

CONCLUSION

You have embarked on a journey that has taken you from the fundamental principles of soapmaking to advanced techniques that bring together artistry, science, and the pleasure of crafting something beautiful with your own hands. As you reach the conclusion of "Crafting Luxurious Soaps: Art, Science, and Scent: Handmade Beauty for Everyday Use," you have reached the end of this journey. In addition to fostering a deeper relationship with the materials and procedures that go into personal care, soapmaking is a skill that has stood the test of time because it enables you to produce luxurious products that can be adapted to your specific needs.

Throughout the entirety of this book, we have investigated the extensive history of soapmaking as well as its development into a contemporary craft that strikes a balance between creativity and practicality. The first thing that we did was investigate the science of saponification, which is the process by which oils and fats are converted into soap through the application of lysine. Because you have gained an understanding of the significance of safety and precision in the handling of ingredients, you are now able to ensure that your soapmaking practice is not only successful but also pleasurable. The ability to master this base opens up a world of possibilities, as you have seen in the wide variety of oils, butter, and additions that are available to create your soaps for certain purposes and preferences.

In addition, the creative side of soapmaking has been a primary focus throughout the entirety of this book. You have learned how to infuse your soaps with your own particular flare and visual appeal, whether it be through the creation of intricate swirls and layers or through the blending of one-of-a-kind essential oil smells. The incorporation of natural components such as botanicals, clays, and exfoliants not only contributes to the aesthetic appeal of your works but also confers additional advantages to the skin. Therefore, soapmaking is a very personal skill that reflects your individuality and tastes because there are an infinite number of color combinations, smell combinations, and texture combinations.

When you make your own soap, you have the power to decide what ingredients are used in the goods that you put on your skin, which is one of the most satisfying components of the process. Handmade soaps provide a natural and environmentally beneficial option in today's society, which is dominated by mass-produced items and other products that are manufactured using synthetic chemicals. By making use of natural, eco-friendly components, you are not only producing high-quality goods, but you are also making a contribution to a lifestyle that is both healthier and more environmentally friendly. An empowering practice that develops consciousness for the environment and personal well-being, making soap by hand is a technique that supports individual empowerment.

As you progress further in your soapmaking adventure, it is important to keep in mind that the process of learning never truly comes to an end. At any given moment, there are fresh methods to investigate, new components to try out, and new concepts to bring into existence. Because of the information that you have learned from this book, you are now equipped with the abilities and the self-assurance necessary to continue making soaps that are not just practical but also functional pieces of beauty. The foundation to create with purpose, care, and creativity is now in your possession, regardless of whether you choose to make soaps as a hobby, for the purpose of giving, or even as a small business endeavor.

When everything is said and done, soapmaking is more than just a craft; it is a practice that offers delight and happiness, both in the process of production and in the usage of the end product. By allowing you to nourish your skin while having the opportunity to enjoy the rewards of your effort, handmade soaps convert ordinary routines into moments of self-care and enjoyment. You are embracing a holistic approach to beauty and well-being when you embrace the art, science, and aroma of soapmaking. This approach is one that embraces the simple joys of handmade crafting rather than focusing on the aesthetics of the finished product.

As you proceed along this path, let your creative abilities develop, your skills become more refined, and your respect for this ageless craft grow. We are grateful that you have chosen to participate in this imaginative investigation of handmade beauty, which is a place where art, science, and fragrance come together in the form of luxury soaps that may be used on a daily basis.

Thank you for buying and reading/ listening to our book. If you found this book useful/ helpful please take a few minutes and leave a review on the platform where you purchased our book. Your feedback matters greatly to us.